I0438714

science for a changing world

Prepared as part of the U.S. Geological Survey Priority Ecosystems Science Initiative

Spatial and Stage-Structured Population Model of the American Crocodile for Comparison of Comprehensive Everglades Restoration Plan (CERP) Alternatives

By Timothy W. Green, Daniel H. Slone, Eric D. Swain, Michael S. Cherkiss, Melinda Lohmann, Frank J. Mazzotti, and Kenneth G. Rice

Open-File Report 2010–1284

U.S. Department of the Interior
U.S. Geological Survey

U.S. Department of the Interior
KEN SALAZAR, Secretary

U.S. Geological Survey
Marcia K. McNutt, Director

U.S. Geological Survey, Reston, Virginia 2010

For product and ordering information:
World Wide Web: http://www.usgs.gov/pubprod
Telephone: 1-888-ASK-USGS

For more information on the USGS—the Federal source for science about the Earth,
its natural and living resources, natural hazards, and the environment:
World Wide Web: http://www.usgs.gov
Telephone: 1-888-ASK-USGS

Suggested citation:
Green, T.W., Slone, D.H., Swain, E.D., and others, 2001, Spatial and Stage-Structured Population Model of the American Crocodile for Comparison of Comprehensive Everglades Restoration Plan (CERP) Alternatives:.U.S. Geological Survey Open-File Report 2010-1284, 57 p.

Contents

Figures

Tables

Conversion Factors and Abbreviations

Multiply	By	To obtain
Length		
centimeter (cm)	0.3937	inch (in.)
meter (m)	3.281	foot (ft)
kilometer (km)	0.6214	mile (mi)
kilometer (km)	0.5400	mile, nautical (nmi)
meter (m)	1.094	yard (yd)
Area		
square meter (m^2)	0.0002471	acre (ac)
Velocity or rate of accumulation		
centimeter per year (cm/yr)	0.3937	inch per year (in./yr)
kilometer per day (km/d)	0.6214	mile per day (mi./d)
Mass		
gram (g)	0.03527	ounce, avoirdupois (oz)

ppt   parts per thousand

Temperature in degrees Celsius (°C) may be converted to degrees Fahrenheit (°F) as follows:
°F=(1.8×°C)+32
Temperature in degrees Fahrenheit (°F) may be converted to degrees Celsius (°C) as follows:
°C=(°F-32)/1.8

Spatial and Stage-Structured Population Model of the American Crocodile for Comparison of Comprehensive Everglades Restoration Plan (CERP) Alternatives

Timothy W. Green[1], Daniel H. Slone[1], Eric D. Swain[2], Michael S. Cherkiss[3], Frank J. Mazzotti[3], Kenneth G. Rice[1]

Abstract

As part of the U.S. Geological Survey Priority Ecosystems Science (PES) initiative to provide the ecological science required during Everglades restoration, we have integrated current regional hydrologic models with American crocodile (*Crocodylus acutus*) research and monitoring data to create a model that assesses the potential impact of Comprehensive Everglades Restoration Plan (CERP) efforts on the American crocodile.

A list of indicators was created by the Restoration Coordination and Verification (RECOVER) component of CERP to help determine the success of interim restoration goals. The American crocodile was established as an indicator of the ecological condition of mangrove estuaries due to its reliance upon estuarine environments characterized by low salinity and adequate freshwater inflow.

To gain a better understanding of the potential impact of CERP restoration efforts on the American crocodile, a spatially explicit crocodile population model has been created that has the ability to simulate the response of crocodiles to various management strategies for the South Florida ecosystem. The crocodile model uses output from the Tides and Inflows in the Mangroves of the Everglades (TIME) model, an application of the Flow and Transport in a Linked Overland/Aquifer Density Dependent System (FTLOADDS) simulator. TIME has the capability to link to the South Florida Water Management Model (SFWMM), which is the primary regional tool used to assess CERP restoration scenarios.

A crocodile habitat suitability index and spatial parameter maps that reflect salinity, water depth, habitat, and nesting locations are used as driving functions to construct crocodile finite rate of increase maps under different management scenarios. Local stage-structured models are integrated with a spatial landscape grid to display crocodile movement behavior in response to changing environmental conditions.

Restoration efforts are expected to affect salinity levels throughout the habitat of the American crocodile. This modeling effort examines how CERP restoration alternatives will affect growth and survival rates of hatchling and juvenile crocodiles, hatchling dispersal to suitable nursery habitat, and relative abundance and distribution in response to changing salinity and water depth for all stage classes of crocodiles. The response of the American crocodile to restoration efforts will provide a quantifiable measure of restoration success. By applying the crocodile model to proposed restoration alternatives

---

[1] USGS Florida Southeastern Ecological Science Center, Gainesville, FL, USA
[2] USGS Florida Water Science Center, Fort Lauderdale, FL, USA
[3] University of Florida IFAS Research and Education Center, Fort Lauderdale, FL, USA

and predicting population responses, we can choose alternatives that approximate historical conditions, enhance habitat for multiple species, and identify future research needs.

Future modeling efforts will include climate change scenarios and will cover an expanded area that includes Biscayne Bay and the Ten Thousand Islands.

Introduction

The American crocodile (*Crocodylus acutus*) is a federally endangered top consumer in southern Florida, imperiled primarily by habitat loss due to expansion of a rapidly growing human population along the coastal areas of Palm Beach, Broward, Miami-Dade, and Monroe Counties (Mazzotti, 1983). This loss of habitat affected the nesting range of crocodiles by restricting nesting to a small area of northeastern Florida Bay and northern Key Largo by the early 1970s (Ogden, 1978; Kushlan and Mazzotti, 1989). When crocodiles were listed as endangered in 1975, few data were available for making informed management decisions. Field and laboratory data suggested that low nesting success, combined with high hatchling mortality, provided a dim prognosis for survival (Dunson, 1970; Evans and Ellis, 1977; Ogden, 1978). Because of their small size, hatchling crocodiles are vulnerable to biotic and abiotic stressors, such as high levels of salinity (Mazzotti and others, 2007). To grow and survive, hatchling crocodiles need to find food and benign environmental conditions (or at least avoid harsh conditions) and avoid predators. Diminished growth rates and increased mortality or dispersal rates have been associated with areas that pose a risk to hatchling crocodiles (Mazzotti, 1999).

Crocodiles now occur in most of the remaining suitable habitat in southern Florida (Mazzotti and others, 2007). Most of the remaining habitat is currently protected in public ownership or located within the boundaries of the Turkey Point Nuclear Power Plant where there is an active program managing for crocodiles. In these areas, further loss of habitat is not an issue. However, questions of potential habitat modification through continued alteration of freshwater flow due to upstream development and potential curtailment of the range of crocodiles need to be addressed. Patterns of nesting and hatchling dispersal, relative abundance and distribution, growth, and survival of crocodiles can provide insight into restoration of coastal ecosystems in southern Florida. Restoring a more natural pattern of freshwater flow is likely to benefit the crocodile population in the long-term (U.S. Fish and Wildlife Service, 1999). Characteristics of flow patterns beneficial for crocodiles include low levels of sheetflow through fringing mangrove swamps that persist well into the dry season. Mid-to late dry season freshwater discharges that raise water levels in the receiving body are hypothesized to disperse prey items, making them less available to crocodiles (Mazzotti, 2007).

Restoration efforts in the Comprehensive Everglades Restoration Plan (CERP) will probably affect salinity levels throughout the habitat of the American crocodile. Reduced freshwater flow has been associated with increased salinity levels in Florida Bay estuaries, a core nesting area of the American crocodile. Although large crocodiles are not significantly affected by high salinity, previous work has shown that high salinity levels increase mortality of hatchlings and juveniles (Moler, 1991; Mazzotti, 1999). The detrimental effects of high salinity on hatchling and juvenile crocodiles have led to the hypothesis that increased freshwater flow to the estuaries will increase the distribution, abundance, and growth of these animals.

The American crocodile was chosen as an indicator species by the Restoration Coordination and Verification (RECOVER) component of CERP to help determine the success of interim restoration goals. Crocodiles were chosen to assess the ecological condition of mangrove estuaries because of their reliance upon estuarine environments characterized by appropriate salinity regimes and adequate freshwater inflows. The desired restoration condition for American crocodiles under CERP is to restore freshwater flow volume and frequency to lower salinities in Florida Bay throughout the hatching period for optimal growth and survival of juvenile crocodiles.

To gain a better understanding of the potential impact of CERP restoration efforts on crocodile populations, a spatially explicit crocodile population model was created that can simulate the south Florida ecosystem under various management strategies. The Comprehensive Everglades Restoration Crocodile Model (CERCM) was constructed using existing research and monitoring data along with expert opinion.

CERCM uses output from the Tides and Inflows in the Mangroves of the Everglades (TIME) model, an application of the Flow and Transport in a Linked Overland/Aquifer Density Dependent System (FTLOADDS) simulator (Wang, 2007). TIME has the capability to link to the South Florida Water Management Model (SFWMM), which is the primary regional tool used to assess CERP restoration scenarios (fig. 1). By applying the crocodile model to proposed restoration alternatives and predicting population responses, we can choose alternatives that approximate historical conditions, enhance habitat for multiple species, and identify future research needs.

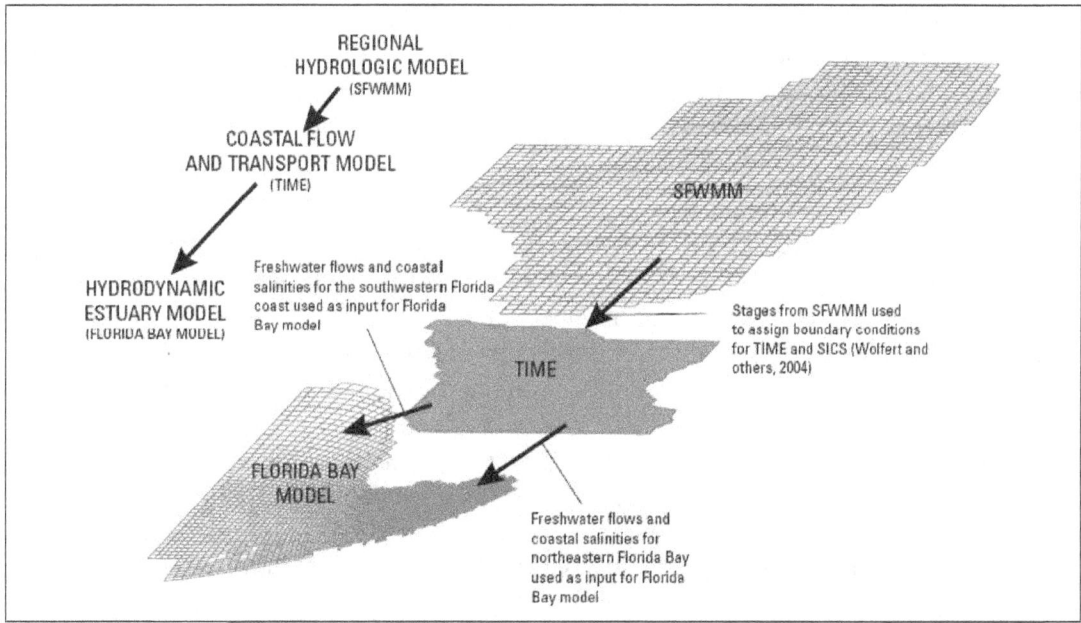

Figure 1. Linkage between models used to simulate various restoration scenarios. SFWMM is South Florida Water Management Model. From Wang and others (2007).

Methods

Model Overview

CERCM is a spatially explicit stage-structured population model that incorporates a structure similar to that used in the Across Trophic Level System Simulation (ATLSS) model of American alligator growth and dispersal (Slone and others, 2003).

The model is based on a 3-dimensional matrix that records the density of each crocodile stage in each 500×500-m modeled area on a daily basis. The model was developed to be stage-based and spatially explicit in order to simultaneously evaluate landscape effects on each life stage of the

American crocodile and predict spatial density patterns and relative changes in population size. Crocodile population parameters are estimated across hydrologic and habitat gradients. The model was created in Matlab (Mathworks, 2008).

Model Structure

The stage structured crocodile population is represented as a 3-dimensional array, $N(i, j, k)$, indexing the number (N) in stage k at spatial location (i, j). Each spatial location is subject to the effects of crocodile parameters relative to habitat and dynamic salinity and water depth conditions. A table of parameters used within the model can be found in Appendix 1.

The crocodile population matrix is structured by stages with a Lefkovitch projection matrix allowing for partial class development within each stage. Crocodile stages within the model are based upon both age and size class with adequate time and growth necessary to advance to the next stage. Unfavorable conditions can result in slower growth rates and additional time spent in a particular stage. Each stage is subject to the same mortality, fecundity, and growth rates. By using a Lefkovitch projection, we are able to identify how hydrologic conditions impact individual stages of development differently and increase the accuracy of information provided to managers.

Constructing the projection matrix at each location provides λ, the largest eigenvalue, which will indicate whether the population will increase ($\lambda > 1$) or decrease ($\lambda < 1$) at each location. This eigenvalue provides information on crocodile population growth and decline over time.

Hydrologic Inputs

To accurately represent the Everglades flows and their respective flow alterations caused by restoration, USGS hydrologists developed a coupled surface-water/ground-water numerical code known as FTLOADDS. This crocodile model uses the application of FTLOADDS to the larger TIME model. This hydrologic model generates salinity and water depth for most of the potential habitat of the American crocodile within Everglades National Park. Future extensions will include the southwestern coastline of Cape Sable, Biscayne Bay and the Ten Thousand Islands.

Previous Habitat Suitability Index (HSI) and individual based crocodile modeling efforts have used the Southern Inland and Coastal Systems (SICS) hydrologic model, an earlier application of FTLOADDS, to acquire salinity and water depth (Swain and others, 2004). Comparisons of TIME simulation results have shown improved capabilities over SICS in the representation of coastal flows due to a more stable numerical representation of coastal creek outlets (Wang and others, 2007). These creeks are prime habitat and dispersal corridors for crocodiles of all stage classes. The spatial extent of TIME also extends beyond the range of SICS, encompassing all of Everglades National Park, including habitat around Cape Sable, where crocodiles have recently been observed in greater numbers.

At this time, the spatial extent of the TIME model does not include the southwestern shoreline of Cape Sable, which has a large number of nesting locations and increased crocodile density and distribution in recent years. Due to the importance of southwestern Cape Sable to the American crocodile population in southern Florida, we extended the boundary of the crocodile model past the TIME boundary to include this area. Values of cells along the existing TIME boundary that did not include open water were extended to adjacent crocodile habitat cells to provide salinity and depth values for all cells that were considered to be potential crocodile habitat. Future TIME model output is expected to expand in spatial extent to cover all of Cape Sable. This output will likely differ from the hydrology used in the domain expansion within this model as complex interactions between interior and coastal hydrologic influences are more fully accounted for. Until that time, crocodile density and distribution along the southwestern part of Cape Sable should be viewed as preliminary output subject to modification in the future.

We also extended the hydrologic spatial extent of the TIME model southward into Florida Bay to include islands where nesting sites were frequently observed. This extension was created by computing the average value of adjacent cells to the north and extending those values southward into Florida Bay to cover the spatial extent of current crocodile nesting locations. This area is only used by females for nesting. Immediately after eggs hatch, adult females and hatchling crocodiles disperse northward (back into the spatial extent of the validated TIME model). Hatchlings disperse northward in search of suitable nursery habitat and females disperse northward in search of more favorable conditions.

Model Environment

The spatial domain of CERCM includes potential crocodile habitat located within the approximately 85 × 75-km domain of the TIME model. TIME is bounded to the north by Tamiami Trail (U.S. Highway 41) and Barron River; to the west by the Gulf of Mexico, to the south by Florida Bay, and to the east by Levee 31N, Levee 31W, Levee C-111, and U.S. Highway 1. The spatial extent of the crocodile model was extended beyond the boundaries of the existing TIME model to include active crocodile nesting locations on islands within Florida Bay and along the southwestern Florida coastline. The spatial extensions include areas along the coastline of Cape Sable, along the coastline north of Lostmans River, and southward into Florida Bay. The southern extension terminates at lat. 25° 4′ 28.1″, long. -80° 38′ 51″ (UTM 2773256.98 535526.982). The spatial domain of the model along with geographic points of reference is shown in figure 2.

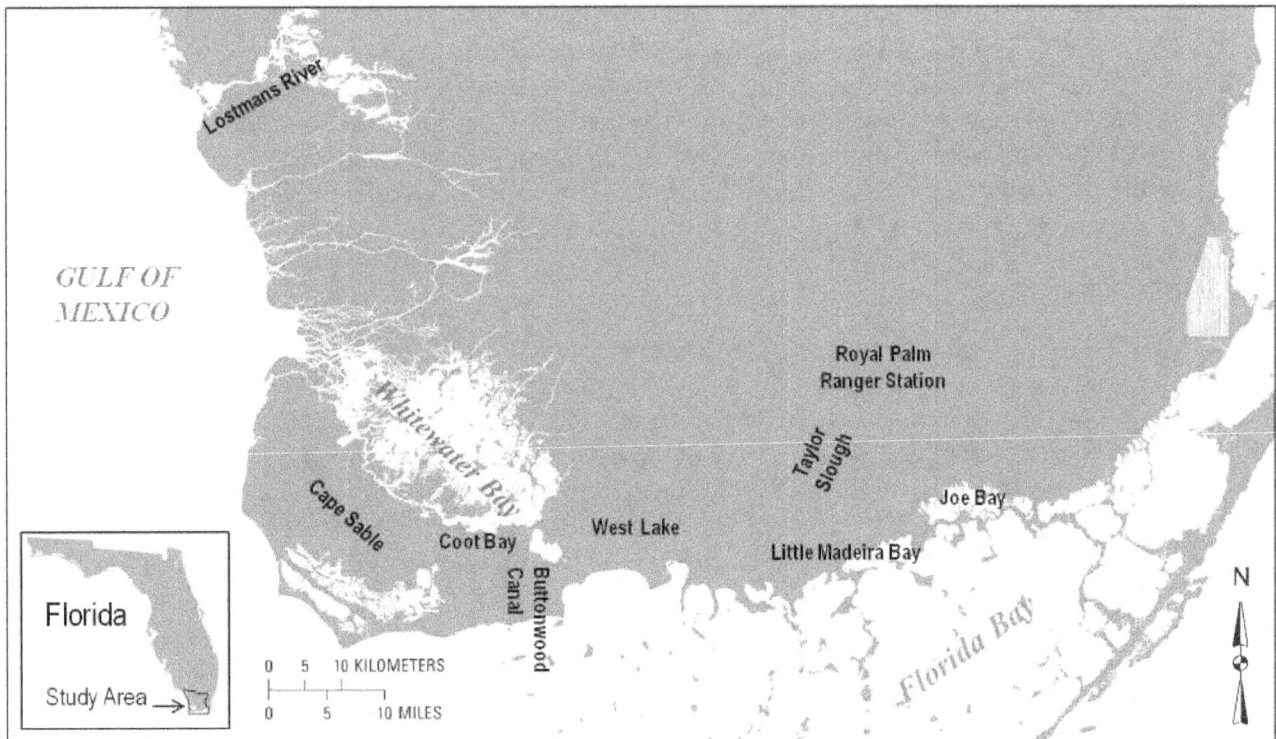

Figure 2.   American crocodile model domain and geographic features.

The model uses a static habitat layer based upon "A Natural History Based Model of Potential Habitat for the American Crocodile" developed by Mazzotti and others (U.S. Geological Survey, written commun. 2006). Potential crocodile habitat is defined to be all natural land cover within the mangrove zone and within 500 m of inland creeks and canals, 100 m inland of the coastal shoreline, and 900 m seaward of the shoreline. The natural land covers included are predominantly mangrove forest (mixed, red, and dwarf), tropical hardwood forest, coastal prairie, coastal marsh, and open water. The land cover types are taken from the USGS Florida Gap Analysis Program (FLGAP) 1993/94 land cover classification. Additional habitat cells were added to the original spatial extent when deemed necessary to aid in crocodile dispersal. This was done by incorporating additional 500-m habitat cells in specific locations to create a corridor between disconnected habitat cells.

Crocodile Interactions with the Environment

The distribution and abundance of estuarine crocodiles is dependent upon the timing, amount, and location of freshwater flow (Dunson and Mazzotti, 1989; Mazzotti and Dunson, 1989). Hatchling and juvenile survival is dependent upon access to freshwater. Several laboratory and field studies have reported a negative relationship between salinity and growth rate in hatchling and juvenile crocodiles (Mazzotti, 2007; Schubert and others, 1996). Decreased growth rates, especially during the first 4 months following hatching, are hypothesized to result in decreased survival rates of hatchling crocodiles (Moler, 1991a; Mazzotti, 1989). Failure to reach a critical mass by the onset of the cooler dry season when dispersal is limited, growth is minimal, and predators are concentrated can result in increased hatchling mortality.

Although hatchlings and juveniles may be the most affected, all stage classes are impacted by hydrologic conditions (Mazzotti 1999; Mazzotti and others 2007b). Crocodiles are reported to occur at the lower end of the available salinity gradient (Mazzotti, 1983, 1999; Brandt and others, 1995; Cherkiss, 1999). The majority of crocodile sightings occur in water with an associated salinity of less than 20 ppt. Crocodile sightings in more saline water are usually females attending nest sites, hatchlings at nest sites, or juveniles likely attempting to avoid adults (Mazzotti and others, 2007).

All stage classes rely upon small demersal fish as a major component of their diet. These prey fish within the mangrove zone are dependent upon a specific range of salinity and water depth (Lorenz, 1999). Crocodile growth and dispersal is linked to the distribution and availability of these small fish.

Basic Model Cycle

The crocodile model runs on a daily time step, the same as used in the TIME model. During each daily time step, every cell within the 28-layer matrix is affected by salinity, water depth, and crowding. Each layer is made up of 184 rows and 176 columns of cells (a total of 32,384 cells per layer). Each cell is representative of a 500-m^2 spatial area. The first 18 layers of the matrix compose the crocodile density map, with each layer representing a different stage of development (table 1). An age class (hatchling, juvenile, subadult, adult male and adult female) may include multiple stages. The more stages there are within an age class, the greater the amount of time crocodiles are likely to remain within that age class, but this time varies with a transfer rate parameter. The remaining ten layers of the matrix represent daily growth and survival conditions. There are five growth layers and five survival layers representing the impact of growth and survival conditions on the different crocodile age classes. Growth and survival parameters are consistent throughout an age class.

Table 1. Crocodile model matrix layers and the relationship between stage and age class

Stage	Age class	Stage number	Layer
Egg		St1	1
Hatchling	Hatchling	St2	2
Small juvenile	Juvenile	St3	3
Large juvenile	Juvenile	St4	4
Subadult stage 1	Subadult	St5	5
Subadult stage 2	Subadult	St6	6
Subadult stage 3	Subadult	St7	7
Subadult stage 4	Subadult	St8	8
Female stage 1	Adult	St9	9
Female stage 2	Adult	St10	10
Female stage 3	Adult	St11	11
Female stage 4	Adult	St12	12
Female stage 5	Adult	St13	13
Male stage 1	Adult	St14	14
Male stage 2	Adult	St15	15
Male stage 3	Adult	St16	16
Male stage 4	Adult	St17	17
Male stage 5	Adult	St18	18
Hatchling Growth			19
Juvenile Growth			20
Subadult Growth			21
Female Growth			22
Male Growth			23
Hatchling Survival			24
Juvenile Survival			25
Subadult Survival			26
Female Survival			27
Male Survival			28

The crocodile model is stage-based; within each stage, crocodiles grow and advance to the next stage, remain within the stage, or die and are removed from the model. Those crocodiles that spend the most amount of time in cells with more favorable conditions for growth have the greatest probability of advancing to the next stage of development. Those that have not grown adequately enough to transfer on the designated day remain in the current stage for another year and are susceptible to all the growth and survival parameters that impact that particular stage of development. The following year, crocodiles once again have the ability to transfer to the next stage of development. The exception to the rule is hatchlings, which have the ability to transfer stages before the onset of the winter dry season. Females within each of the adult female stages have the ability to produce eggs but are influenced by a fecundity vector in which the oldest and youngest females have a lower probability of reproductive success.

Survival

Hatchling and juvenile survival is influenced by salinity, growth rate, cannibalism from older crocodiles, and distance to suitable nursery habitat. Subadult and adult survival is not influenced by salinity. Appendix 2 provides a table of salinity equations used within the model.

Survival parameters represent potential survival under optimal environmental conditions (table 2). Moler (1991) estimated an average first year survival rate of 20.4 percent for the 1979-88 period. These rates ranged from 42.9 percent in 1980 to 6.8 percent in 1987. The large difference in annual survival rates was thought to be a result of environmental conditions and the impact of those conditions on hatchling growth rates. First year survival was 29.6 percent when the crocodiles were able to grow to 42-43 cm (200 g) during the first 3-4 months following hatching. Survival dropped to 10.1 percent when crocodiles did not reach that size.

Table 2. Crocodile survival rate parameters.

[Values represent optimum annual survival rates in the absence of other modeled mortality factors]

Stage	Survival rate parameter	Data source
Hatchling	0.10	Mazzotti (1999); Moler (1991)
Juvenile	0.70	Moler (1991)
Subadult	0.85	Moler (1991)
Adult	0.99	Moler (1991); Kushlan and Mazzotti (1989)

Within the model, the majority of hatchlings will only remain in the hatchling stage during the first 4 months. Hatchlings have the ability to advance to the juvenile stage 117 days after hatching. In the juvenile stage, maximum survival rates are substantially higher. Hatchlings that advance to the juvenile stage after 117 days increase their maximum annualized survival rate from 10 to 70 percent. Crocodiles that grow fast enough to advance to the next stage have a maximum potential survival rate of 36.5 percent within the first year. A 10 percent annualized survival rate is equal to an 82.5 percent monthly survival rate. A 70 percent fall monthly survival rate was documented for hatchlings in Everglades National Park (Mazzotti and others, 2009), where conditions can be harsh and some percentage of hatchlings probably disperses to remote regions where they are unable to be recaptured. First year survival rates of crocodiles in Everglades National Park were reported to be only 1.5 percent (Mazzotti and others, 2007).

Moler (1991) documented that crocodile survival increased greatly during the second year to 64.9 percent. Survival of crocodiles older than 5 years in age exceeds 80 percent and likely approaches 100 percent because crocodiles lack natural predators. Most reported deaths of older crocodiles are human induced (Kushlan and Mazzotti, 1989).

Effect of Salinity on Survival

Because of their small size, hatchling crocodiles are vulnerable to biotic and abiotic stressors. Laboratory and field studies have shown a negative relationship between salinity and survival rates in hatchling and juvenile crocodiles in Florida (Mazzotti, 1983; Mazzotti and Dunson, 1984; Moler, 1991). Hatchling and juvenile survival is negatively affected by salinities above 20 ppt, unlike adult and subadult survival, which are not influenced by salinity. The survival function used in this model was adapted from the relationship developed by Mazzotti and others (2009b) for use in a crocodile HSI. In this function, salinity below 20 ppt does not affect crocodile survival rates, whereas salinity above 40 ppt has the maximum negative influence on hatchlings and juveniles (fig. 3).

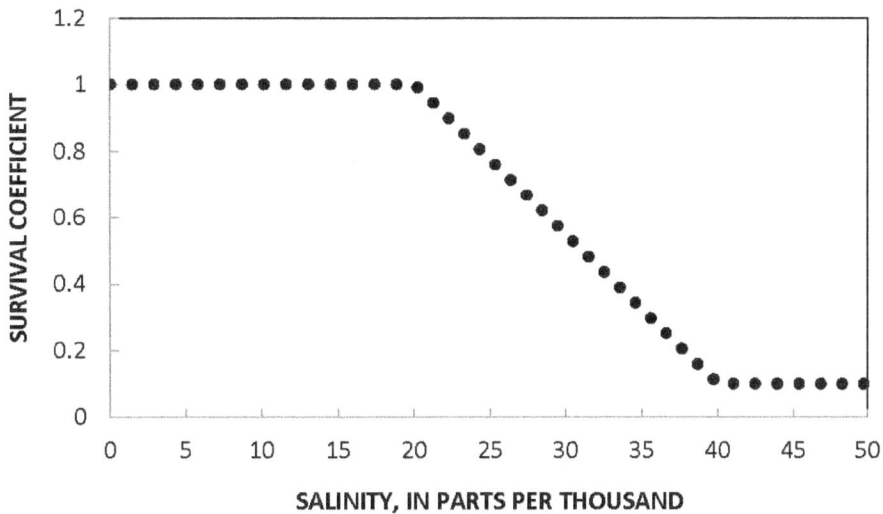

Figure 3. Impact of salinity on hatchling and juvenile American crocodile survival.

Effect of Growth Rate on Survival

Crocodiles greatly increase their tolerance to seawater exposure during the first 3-4 months of rapid growth (Mazzotti and Dunson, 1984). Moler (1991), working in areas with higher survival rates than Everglades National Park, reported that in years when crocodiles attained a mass of 200 g by December, first-year survival averaged 29.6 percent, compared to 10.1 percent when mass was less than 200 g. After 117 days, the probability of survival for those hatchlings that have grown rapidly within the model increases from 10 percent to 70 percent. On average, approximately 90 percent of hatchlings within the model grow fast enough to increase their chances of survival during the winter dry season when salinity concentrations are high, food is low in abundance, and predators are relatively concentrated.

Density-Dependent Survival

Aggressive interactions between different size classes are hypothesized to have an impact on crocodilian population dynamics and be a dominant driver regulating population growth (Nichols and others, 1976; Polis and Myers, 1985; Hutton, 1989). Richards and Wasilewsiki (2003) found six microchips from younger crocodiles in the stomach of a 4-ft (1.2 m) subadult crocodile living in cooling canals around Turkey Point. Density-dependent cannibalism may play a role in the Cape Sable population where much of the best crocodile habitat is found in canals.

Survival of hatchlings and juveniles is affected by the density of subadult and adult crocodiles within the same cell. This crowding of larger crocodiles is considered to be the sum of the probability of adult and subadult occupancy in a given cell. Hatchling and juvenile survival decreases as the density of subadult and adult crocodiles in a cell increases (fig. 4). A cell with an occupancy value of one or greater begins to have a negative influence on hatchling and juvenile survival. This value is meant to symbolize a density of 2 crocodiles per linear km because crocodile habitat within most cells for which density dependence may become an issue consists of coastal creeks and canals. Linear kilometers are the measurement used in spotlight surveys to determine population density. A cell with a density of 2 or more crocodiles has the maximum negative influence, and symbolizes a value of 4 or more crocodiles per linear km. Rarely do spotlight surveys document crocodile densities that exceed 4 crocodiles per linear km. Without a density-dependent relationship, the crocodile subpopulation on Cape Sable grows quite large in comparison to the subpopulation of crocodiles in northeastern Florida Bay.

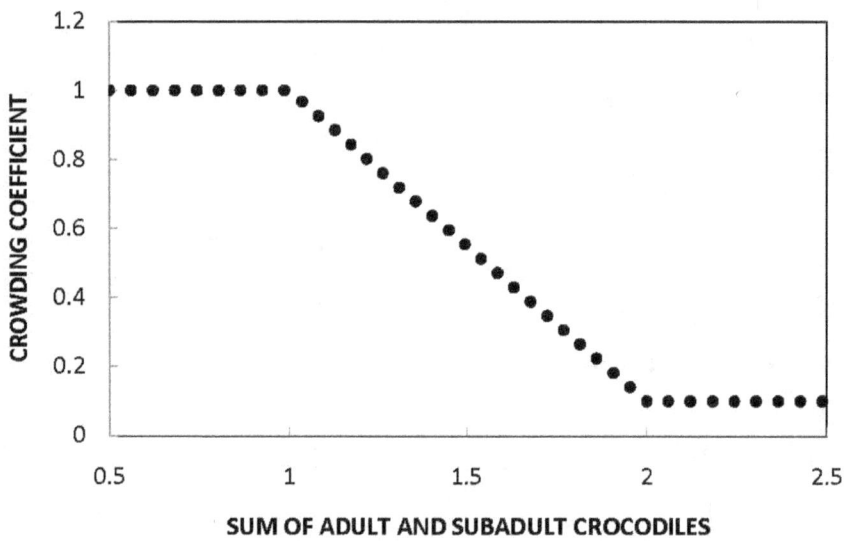

Figure 4.   Impact of adult and subadult crowding on American crocodile hatchling and juvenile survival.

In recent years, crocodile density and distribution has been increasing around Cape Sable, and this relationship may need to be adjusted following future monitoring results and future extension of the TIME model to more accurately account for hydrologic conditions on the southwestern part of Cape Sable. At this time, it is unknown how large the crocodile population on Cape Sable will continue to grow and at what level density-dependent interactions will have larger impacts. With much of the occupied Cape Sable habitat in and around canals, density-dependant interactions may be a large factor in regulating population size. Further research and monitoring of density-dependent relationships within the American crocodile population in southern Florida would provide a greater capacity to accurately predict future population sizes around Cape Sable.

Effect of Distance to Nursery Habitat on Survival

Survival of hatchling crocodiles appears to decrease as the distance that hatchlings must travel to find nursery habitat with suitable salinities increases (Moler, 1991a; Mazzotti, 1999). Suitable nursery habitat is defined as an area that is moderately saline (0-20 ppt), has abundant food sources, has places to hide from predators, and is protected from wind and wave action. Shoreline nests in Everglades National Park may be kilometers away from suitable nursery habitat. Dispersal distances of this length increase the risk of predation and expose hatchling crocodiles to harsh environmental conditions for long periods of time as they search out suitable nursery habitat, decreasing their chances for survival (Mazzotti and others, 2007). Moler (1991b) documented increased hatchling survival estimates in the

Florida Keys in areas where nursery habitat was close to nesting sites and mortality from predators may have been relatively low.

Growth

Low salinity and adequate availability of prey is associated with higher growth rates of young crocodiles (Mazzotti, 1999; Moler 1991a). Growth rates of hatchling and juvenile crocodiles are influenced by salinity and water depth at each spatial location.

Lorenz (2003) determined that the availability of prey for wading birds was a function of water depth and salinity. Mazzotti and others (2009b) incorporated these conclusions into an American crocodile HSI model, taking into account that the American crocodile is capable of feeding in creeks and ponds at depths greater than those of wading birds. In the current model, we used an adaptation of the prey availability equation that was developed for the crocodile HSI, where optimum prey concentration occurred on dry flats and availability of prey fell below the minimum level for full survival in water deeper than 12.5 cm. One limitation of the TIME hydrologic model was the accuracy of shallow water depth estimates. Taking this into account, as well as the distribution of crocodiles found during spotlight surveys from 2004-2008, the depth at which crocodiles would be able to find a minimum availability of prey fish was increased in the model from 12.5 to 25 cm. The impact of water depth on growth is shown in figure 5.

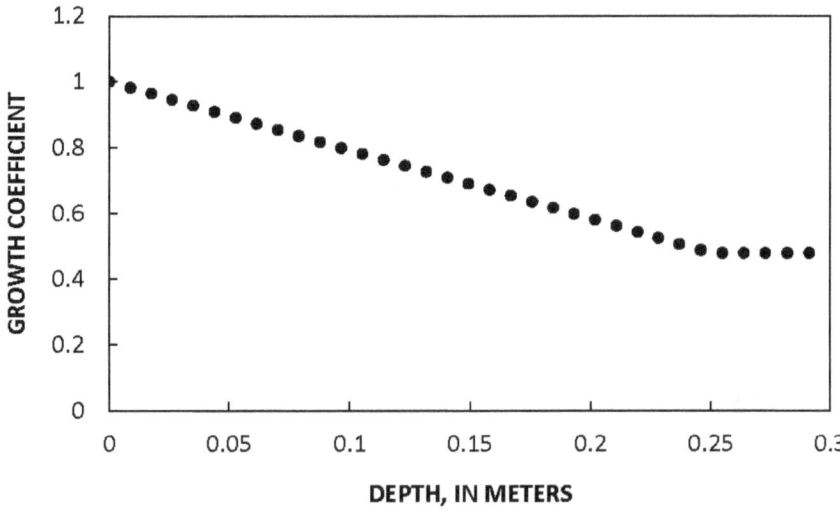

Figure 5.   Impact of depth on growth of hatchling and juvenile American crocodiles.

Resident fish assemblages decrease in abundance and mean size when salinity exceeds 5-8 ppt (Lorenz, 1997, 1999, 2000). Mazzotti and Dunson (1984) found that even with a constant food supply, changing salinities affected crocodile growth rates. Larger crocodiles have a lower rate of mass loss when exposed to high salinities than smaller crocodiles. Crocodiles less than 200 g had a significantly greater mass loss when exposed to high salinities. The relatively rapid growth rate of *C. acutus*, compared to other crocodilians (Mazzotti, 1983), generally results in hatchlings being able to reach 200 g by October-December while environmental conditions are favorable. Reaching this mass by the onset of the dry season when salinities are high and temperatures are cold give young crocodiles a better chance for survival.

Salinity has an impact on hatchling and juvenile growth rates as well as resident prey fish assemblages. Two functions derived from the crocodile HSI are used to measure the impact of salinity on growth, depending on the time of year (fig. 6 and 7). These coefficients for prey fish production at times of both high and low water levels were derived from a predictive model for fish abundance (Lorenz et at., 1997; Lorenz, 1999; Lorenz, 2000). Development of this model consisted of a two-step analysis of an extensive multivariate database that consisted of estimates of fish biomass data collected in Florida Bay and complementary estimates of daily salinity and water-level data (Lorenz, 2003).

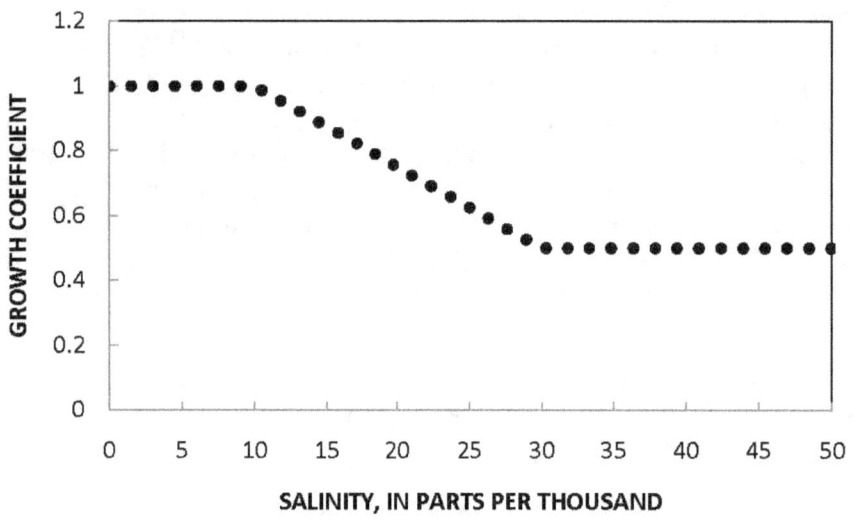

Figure 6.   Impact of salinity on growth of hatchling and juvenile American crocodiles under high water conditions.

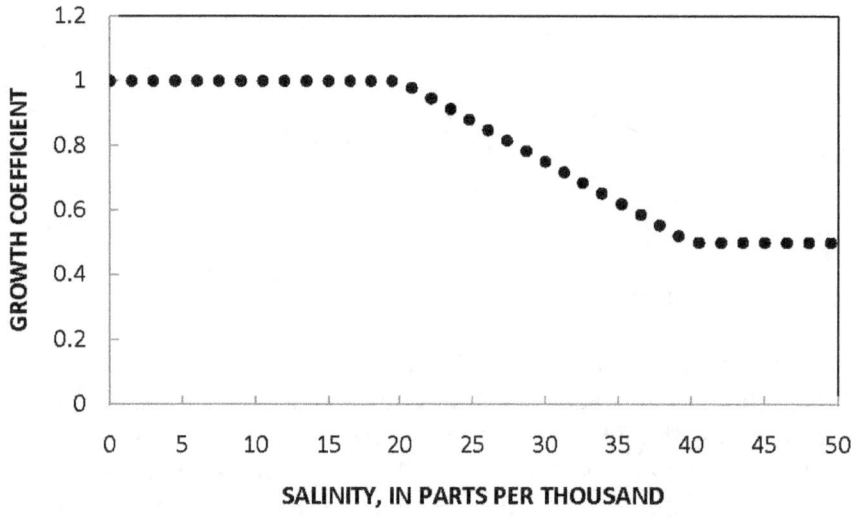

Figure 7.   Impact of salinity on growth of hatchling and juvenile American crocodiles under low water conditions.

High water conditions are considered to be those times of higher water levels during the wet season (Aug.-Dec.). Low water conditions are considered to be those times of lower water levels during the dry season (Jan.-July).

Adult crocodiles, being able to tolerate a higher range of salinities and feed on a greater variety of prey than juveniles, are not affected by these growth constraints and grow at a constant rate. Female growth rates, however, will have an impact on female fecundity and the total number of eggs that are produced each year at individual nest sites.

Stage Transfer

Growth rates determine the rate at which crocodiles transfer to the next stage within the model. Adult stages include a male stage and a female stage. Stage transfer occurs for all stage classes in August when hatchlings are emerging from eggs (fig. 8). Those crocodiles that have maintained the highest growth rates have a greater chance of transferring to the next stage of development at this time. Those that do not transfer will remain in the current stage for another year and be susceptible to all the growth and survival parameters that impact that particular stage of development.

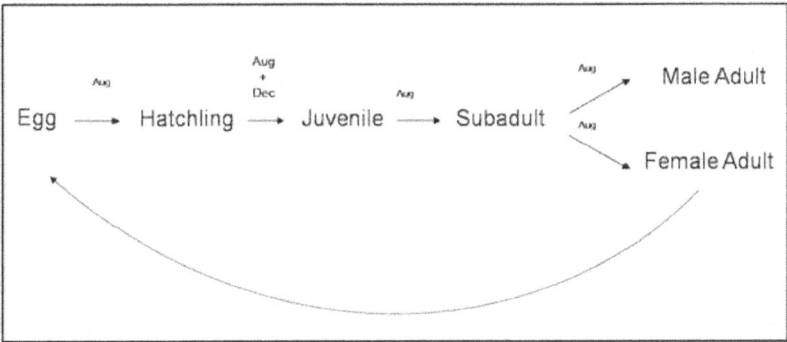

Figure 8.   Stage transfer diagram

Because hatchlings are most susceptible to mortality from high salinity in the first 3-4 months following hatching, there will be an early opportunity for hatchlings to transfer to the juvenile stage in mid-December if they have maintained adequate growth rates. This will increase the survival of larger hatchlings residing in favorable habitat during the winter dry season when salinity is high, dispersal is limited, and predators are relatively concentrated.

Dispersal

Each stage has the ability to disperse daily in response to changing environmental conditions (salinity and water depth). Dispersal occurs on a daily time step between March 1 (julian day 60) and December 1 (julian day 335). Outside of this time period, crocodiles do not disperse within the model because crocodiles remain in localized areas, eating and growing little, during winter months (Kushlan and Mazzotti, 1989; Moler, 1991a).

Dispersal is undertaken using a discrete spatial convolution model of the form:

$$N_{t+1}(x,y) = \sum_{i=1}^{n}\sum_{j=1}^{n} k_s(x-i, y-i) * (N_t(i,j))$$

where * is the convolution operator.

The dispersal kernel is a 3×3 matrix $k_s(i, j)$ that is applied to the entire crocodile density map $N(y, x)$ at each time step for each crocodile stage, s. The dispersal filter is directed toward attractive sources using dispersal kernel functions shaped for each stage based on factors of salinity, water depth, crowding factors, and stage specific dispersal rates (app. 2), giving crocodiles the ability to disperse into favorable adjoining cells. The result is a rearrangement of the population from dispersal sources to attracting sites, driven by changing hydrologic conditions. Because the same dispersal kernels are applied to the growth and survival layers, crocodiles retain the history of the cells where they were previously living.

Adult and subadult crocodiles are rarely found in the open waters of Florida Bay outside of the breeding season, during which it is likely only nesting females passing through to find suitable nesting locations (Dunson and Mazzotti, 1989). To keep a large proportion of adults from dispersing southward into Florida Bay when salinity and water depth conditions are favorable, the dispersal submodel includes an inland habitat map that decreases the probability adult and subadult crocodiles will enter open water exposed to wind and wave action. This dispersal map was created in ArcMap 9.3 (ESRI, 2008) using a proximity analysis to inland habitat.

Rate of Dispersal

American crocodiles are known to disperse across great distances. Crocodiles tagged as hatchlings have been recovered as far as 112 km away (Moler, 1991a). Moler (1991b) reported that three hatchlings covered a distance of over 8 km within a 2-month period, and juveniles were documented covering distances up to 13 km. Richards (2003) reported hatchlings traveling up to 2 km/d. Hatchling and juvenile movement is an important mechanism of dispersal. Soon after hatching, crocodiles begin to disperse toward suitable "nursery habitat" where salinity is low (0-20 ppt), wind and wave action are minimal, and there is an abundant food supply (Mazzotti and others, 2007).

Hatchlings that emerge from shoreline nests in Florida Bay often have to travel several kilometers to find suitable nursery habitat (Mazzotti, 2007). Greater dispersal distance through unfavorable habitat exposes hatchlings to prolonged periods of harsh environmental conditions, reducing growth and survival.

The rate of dispersal is different for each size class, and each dispersal kernel is weighted accordingly by changing the probability that a crocodile will remain in its home cell rather than disperse to an adjoining cell. In one model year, the majority of crocodiles within all size classes remain within 10 km of the cell they were in at the beginning of the year (table 3).

Table 3. Annual dispersal rates for crocodile stage classes.
[km, kilometer]

Size class	% within 10 km	% in center cell
Hatchlings	75.5	0.093
Young juveniles	94.65	0.2
Older juveniles and subadults	75.5	0.093
Adults	87.7	0.14

Hatchling crocodiles are quick to disperse from nest sites to find suitable "nursery" habitat. Once that nursery habitat is found, young juvenile crocodiles are less likely to disperse great distances until they grow a bit larger. Older juveniles and subadults have a greater propensity for long distance dispersal as they try to avoid adults and search out new habitat. Adults, while not sedentary, are more likely to remain within their established home range. In a radio-telemetry study of crocodiles, Mazzotti (1983) tracked a subadult female that was found to move more frequently and have a larger minimal activity range than adults. The dispersal phase of large juveniles and subadult crocodiles may be an integral part of the population dynamics of *C. acutus* and other crocodilians (Thorbjarnarson, 1989).

Reproduction and Female Dispersal to Nesting Locations

All adult female crocodiles in the model have the potential to reproduce. Mean clutch size of *C. acutus* in Florida is 39 eggs with an 82 percent probability that eggs are fertile (Mazzotti, 2007). In the model, this was represented by using a starting clutch size of 39 eggs and applying a fecundity vector [0.71, .085, 1, 0.85, 0.67] to lower the fecundity of very young and very old females compared to middle-aged females. This resulted in an average of 32 fertile eggs per clutch. Female growth rates have an overall impact on reproductive success within the model in that higher growth rates (the result of greater food intake) lead to higher fecundity.

Individual female crocodiles return to the same nest sites during successive years (Ogden, 1978). In this model, all females disperse toward the closest nest sites at the beginning of the nesting season irrespective of water depth or salinity. Potential nest sites include all those nesting locations that have been documented during annual surveys. The nest dispersal map was created in ArcMap using a proximity analysis with a 10 km maximum distance. All documented nest sites except the most northern site on the southwestern coast of Florida were within 10 km of another nest.

Females remain at nest sites until the end of the nesting season. Once eggs have hatched, adult females leave the nest sites and return to more favorable habitat (Ogden, 1978). Dispersal away from nest sites is based upon salinity and water depth conditions using the same dispersal functions used by adult crocodiles throughout the rest of the year.

Model Initialization and Nesting Decisions

Initialization runs began with all crocodiles in each stage originating from historical nest locations. The model was then allowed to run until the population size approached carrying capacity to establish a baseline crocodile density map that would be used for subsequent model runs.

In the current version of this model, nest sites were chosen to be static in order to better determine the implications of CERP restoration on the current distribution of crocodiles within localized regions of northeastern Florida Bay and Cape Sable that are currently inhabited. Running this model with dynamic nesting patterns based upon potential nesting habitat that had not been historically used by crocodiles would allow a percentage of the crocodile population to spread northward along the southwestern coast of Florida where successful nest sites have yet to be documented. Although this expansion is likely a realistic scenario given time and a growing crocodile population, it would have made it more difficult to fully assess the changes in abundance and distribution in response to CERP restoration alternatives on the current distribution of the crocodile population inhabiting southern Florida.

Density-dependent impacts on mortality, limited dispersal abilities, and limited nesting locations keep the population from growing very large or expanding to the north in this version of the model. Using historic nesting sites limits the crocodile population size and distribution to areas currently inhabited by crocodiles in southern Florida. Future model output, including climate change scenarios, will include a probabilistic and dynamic nest map in order to predict where crocodiles may disperse in the future in response to changing hydrologic conditions.

Sensitivity Analysis

A sensitivity analysis was performed for 50 years of model output, from year 50 to year 100, in a 100-year run of randomly-chosen years, where the same set of years was used each time. After 50 years of model output, crocodile population growth had stabilized, with stable, bounded fluctuations in crocodile abundance and distribution (fig. 9). The spatial extent of the sensitivity analysis was a 17.5 × 24.5-km map that included the area around Madeira Bay that was influenced by the hydrology of Taylor Slough. Crocodile habitat within this area experienced some of the greatest hydrologic changes in the model from CERP restoration alternatives.

This is a deterministic model in which every set of variables is uniquely determined by parameters within the model. Hatchling and juvenile survival in response to changing salinity conditions were the most sensitive parameters within the model. Changes in hatchling and juvenile survival rates had a substantial impact on the overall crocodile population size, abundance, and distribution.

Baseline conditions used for comparison during the sensitivity analysis included an annual hatchling survival rate of 0.1 and an annual juvenile survival rate of 0.7 (app. 2). Salinity below 20 ppt did not influence hatchling and juvenile survival. Salinity above 40 ppt had the maximum negative influence.

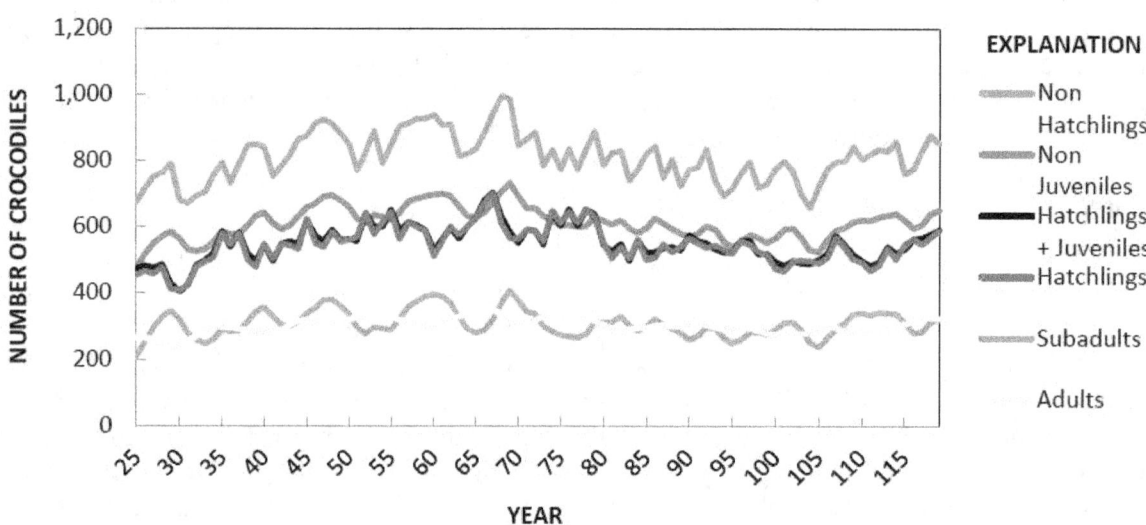

Figure 9.   Fluctuations in the number of American crocodiles in different stages under baseline conditions.

Hatchling Survival Rate Changes

The effect on the crocodile population to relative changes in hatchling survival rates is shown in figure 10. Population density of all age classes increased with increasing hatchling survival rate, but the effect was most pronounced on the younger life stages. The hatchling survival rates used in the sensitivity analysis were 0.01, 0.03, 0.05, 0.1, 0.2, 0.3, and 0.4.

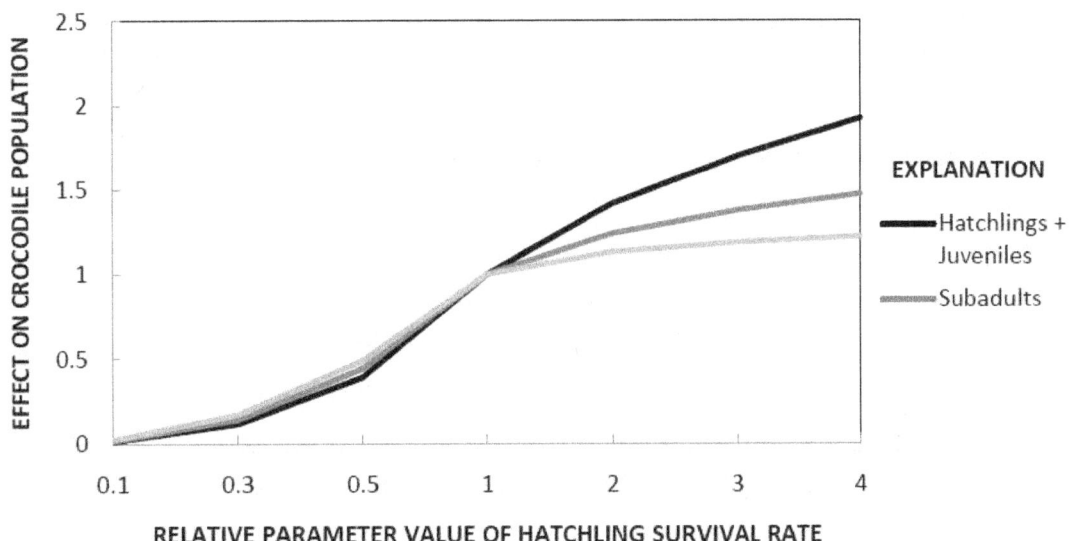

Figure 10.   Percent change in American crocodile population size compared to percent change in hatchling survival rate.

Juvenile Survival Rate Changes

The effect on the crocodile population to relative changes in juvenile survival rates is shown in figure 11. Population density of all age classes increased with increasing juvenile survival rate, but the effect was most pronounced on the subadults—the stage immediately following juveniles. The juvenile survival rates used in the sensitivity analysis were 0.4, 0.5, 0.6, 0.7, 0.8, and 0.9.

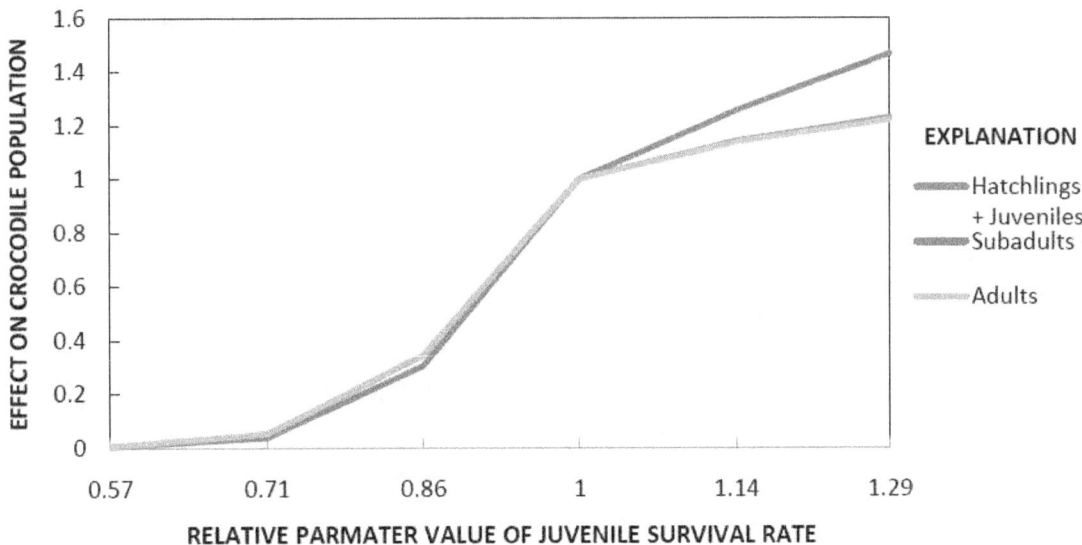

Figure 11.   Effect of the relative change in the juvenile survival rate on the size of the American crocodile population.

The crocodile population was sensitive to changes in hatchling and juvenile survival rates. These survival rates had a large impact on the potential crocodile population size, abundance, and distribution. Considering that first year survival rates have been observed to range from an average of 1.5 percent (Mazzotti and Cherkiss, 2003) to 20.4 percent (Moler, 1991a) depending upon location and environmental conditions, additional research and monitoring efforts will continue to be useful to gain greater insights into the factors affecting hatchling and juvenile survival. The large fluctuation in hatchling and juvenile survival is believed to be the result of distance to nursery habitat, predators, salinity, and prey availability.

Changes in Influence of Salinity on Hatchling and Juvenile Crocodiles

Response to salinity was a highly sensitive parameter within the crocodile model. Lowering the salinity threshold for hatchling and juvenile crocodiles from 40 to 30 ppt resulted in a population decline of 98 percent for all stages. This result indicates that there are few areas with salinity concentrations below 30 ppt within the area considered in the spatial extent of the sensitivity analysis. Crocodiles in northeastern Florida Bay are surviving in water where salinity is frequently above 30 ppt. Although unlikely, if salinity were to increase from the 30- 40 ppt range normally observed in northeastern Florida Bay to 40-50 ppt, a similar population crash to the one shown in figure 12 could be possible. In contrast, increasing the salinity threshold from 40-50 ppt had virtually no effect on the population size.

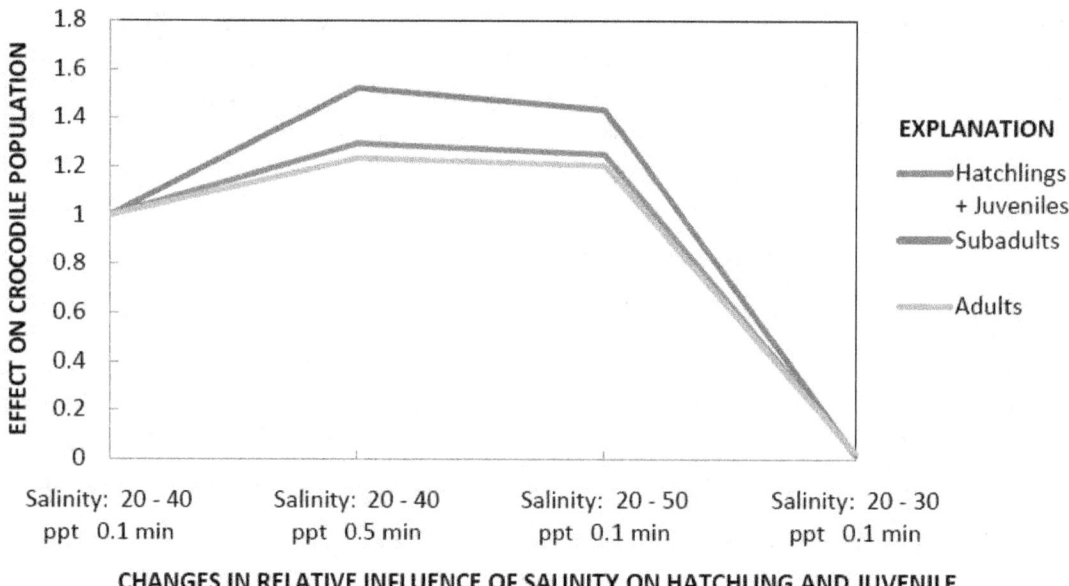

CHANGES IN RELATIVE INFLUENCE OF SALINITY ON HATCHLING AND JUVENILE CROCODILES

Figure 12.   Percent change in the American crocodile population size based on different survival parameters for hatchling and juvenile survival based upon salinity.

Results

Crocodile population size, density, and distribution were compared using two CERP scenarios (CERP0 and CERP2050) that were evaluated using the TIME model. CERP0 was the case that incorporated all planned changes and CERP2050 was the case that delineated conditions in year 2050 if no system changes were made. These two CERP scenarios were compared against scenario R158, which was used to calibrate the TIME model using the 2×2 South Florida Water Management Model (SFWMM) and represents existing conditions from 1996 to 2000.

There were fluctuations in population size from year to year depending upon hydrologic conditions. During some years, the CERP0 scenario resulted in the greatest population size, but for the most part, overall population size across all crocodile stages was greatest under the CERP2050 scenario. There was a 2 percent decrease in average hatchling and juvenile population size under CERP0 compared to CERP2050. There was a 3.5 percent decrease in average subadult population size and an average decrease of 3.2 percent in adult population size under CERP0 compared to CERP2050. This decrease in population size under CERP0 conditions was mostly a result of consistently higher salinities under CERP0 for areas around Buttonwood canal and Coot Bay (including Bear Lake and Mud Lake to the southwest of Coot Bay).

On average, the total crocodile population size was smallest under CERP0 conditions across all stages, but regional density and distribution fluctuated. This fluctuation was most evident in northeastern Florida Bay where CERP restoration appeared to have either a positive impact or no impact. Although the greatest changes in total population size may have been in response to natural annual variation in hydrologic conditions, CERP implementation did appear to have a measurable impact on crocodile abundance and distribution in the model.

In 100 randomly selected years of model output using 1996-2000 hydrologic conditions , several standout years warranted further examination (fig. 13). Year 39 had the lowest hatchling, juvenile, and adult population sizes, but the subadult population was robust. In year 39, crocodiles in northeastern Florida Bay fared worse under CERP0 conditions. By contrast, year 80 had the highest hatchling and juvenile population sizes, and crocodiles in northeastern Florida Bay fared better under CERP0 conditions. By comparing these two output years we were able to gain a better understanding of the differences between changing crocodile density and distribution as a result of natural annual variation in hydrologic conditions and differences that came about as a result of CERP implementation.

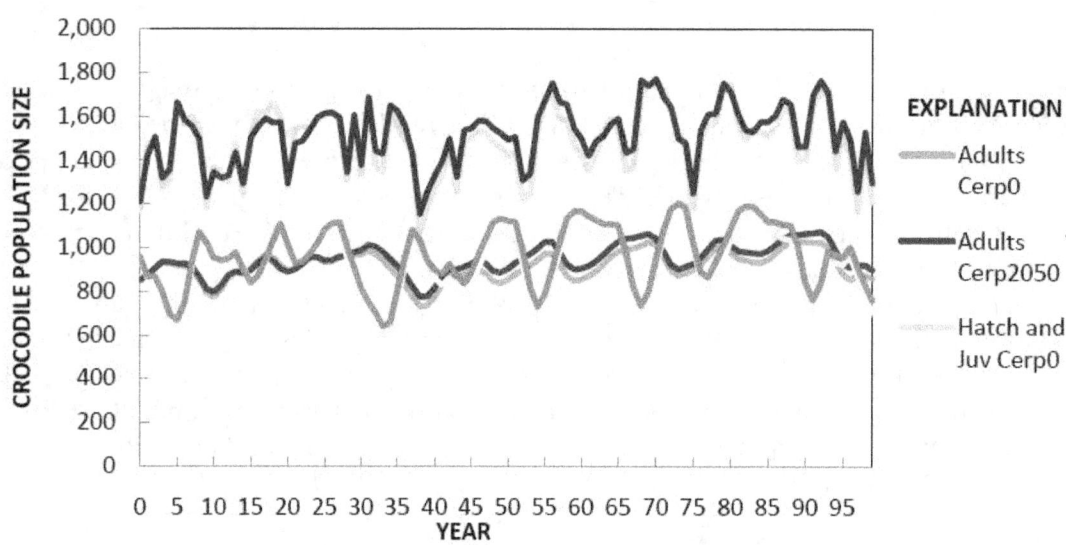

Figure 13. Differences between the annual American crocodile population size by stage under CERP0 and CERP2050 conditions.

The largest decreases in hatchling and juvenile population size were in response to hydrologic conditions during 1996, which was the selected condition in year 39 of the random model run. Annual precipitation for 1996 was the lowest on record (41.01 in.) at the Royal Palm Ranger Station for the period of CERP model output (1996-2000) (table 4). Royal Palm Ranger Station maintained continuous precipitation records in closest proximity to northeastern Florida Bay. The dry conditions in 1996 likely resulted in high salinities for northeastern Florida Bay and had a negative impact on hatchling and juvenile crocodile survival. By contrast, 1997-99 precipitation records from Royal Palm Ranger Station exceeded 58 in/yr. Year 80 used the hydrologic condition from 1999, which was the wettest year in the available record.

Table 4. Precipitation records from the Southeastern Regional Climate Center for Royal Palm Ranger Station, Florida.

[Monthly precipitation recorded in inches]

Year	Jan.	Feb.	Mar.	Apr.	May	Jun.	Jul.	Aug.	Sep.	Oct.	Nov.	Dec.	Total
1996	0	0.7	1.66	2.9	7.89	9.38	3.29	7.96	6.16	9.39	0.32	0.74	41.01
1997	2.33	0.61	1.66	0	5.02	20.9	6.6	6.86	8.05	3.64	2.36	0	58.03
1998	2.19	5.2	4.97	0.02	6.13	2.28	5.29	6.39	18.16	2.82	7.35	0.6	61.4
1999	3.16	0.29	0.69	0.82	5.69	6.45	4.19	11.19	14.18	14.13	2.57	1.47	64.83
2000	0.56	1.49	3.37	4.21	1.37	8.75	6.28	7.66	7.08	6.91	0.29	1.9	49.87
2001	0.44	0	2.99	3.06	4.6	8.69	6.71	12.88	11.14	5.98	1.31	2.12	59.92
2002	1.36	2.26	1.63	0.75	8.82	13.54	11.68	4.77	4.12	0.83	1.97	1.06	52.79

In Appendix 3, output from year 39 and year 80 are provided for the combined hatchling and juvenile stage, the subadult stage, adult stage, and all stages combined. The density and distribution output for each stage portrays these differences as being quite subtle, but by using percent change maps we were able to show these differences in greater detail (figs. 14-29).

20

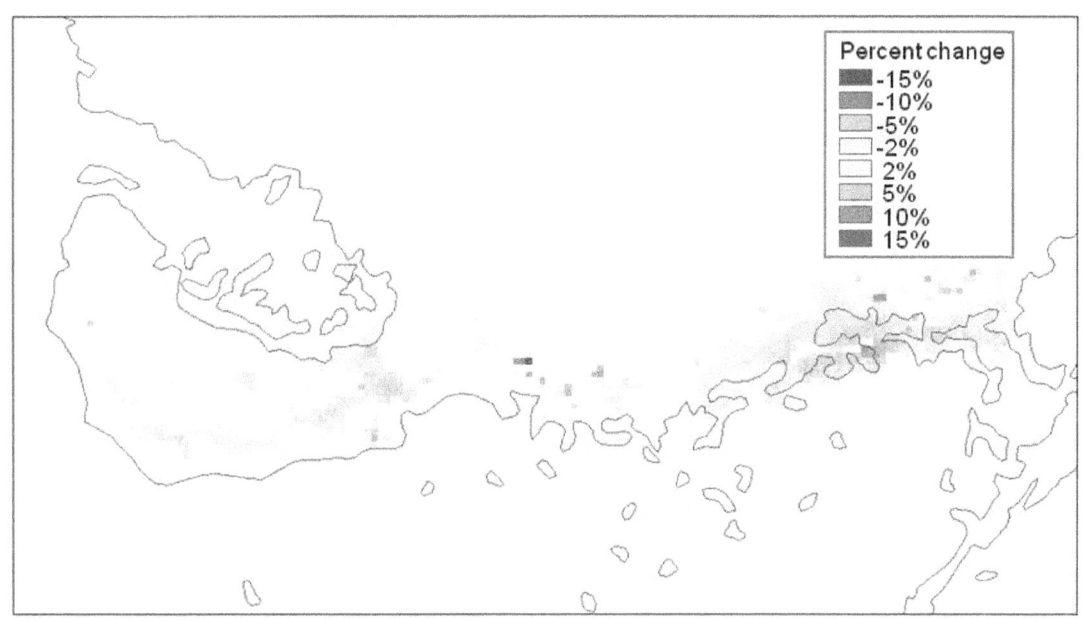

Figure 14. Percent change between total American crocodile density and distribution under CERP0 conditions compared to CERP2050 conditions (Year 39).

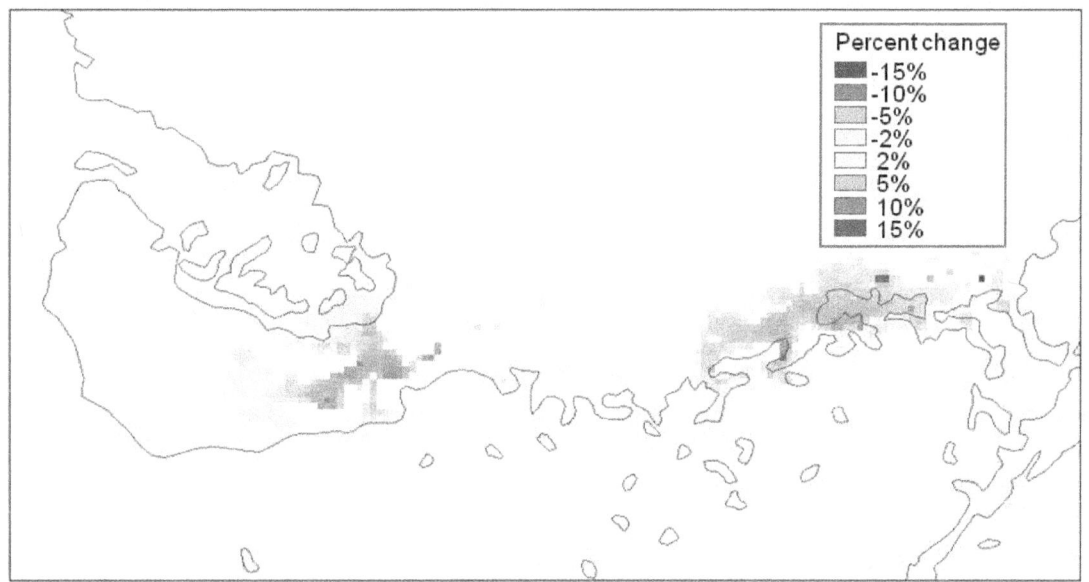

Figure 15. Percent change between total American crocodile density and distribution under CERP0 conditions compared to CERP2050 conditions (Year 80).

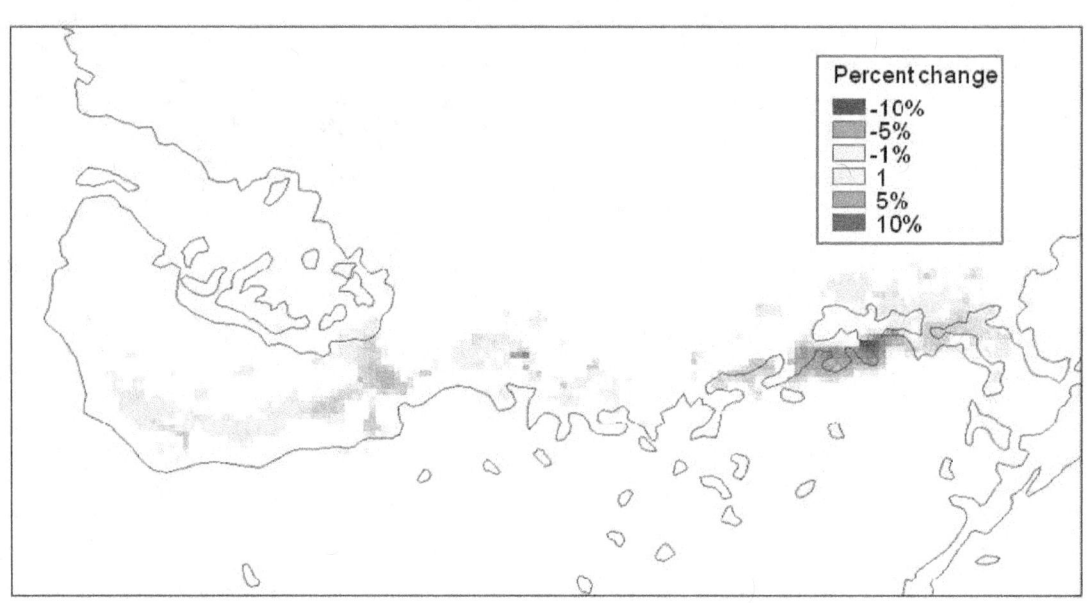

Figure 16. Percent change between hatchling American crocodile density and distribution under CERP0 conditions compared to CERP2050 conditions (Year 39).

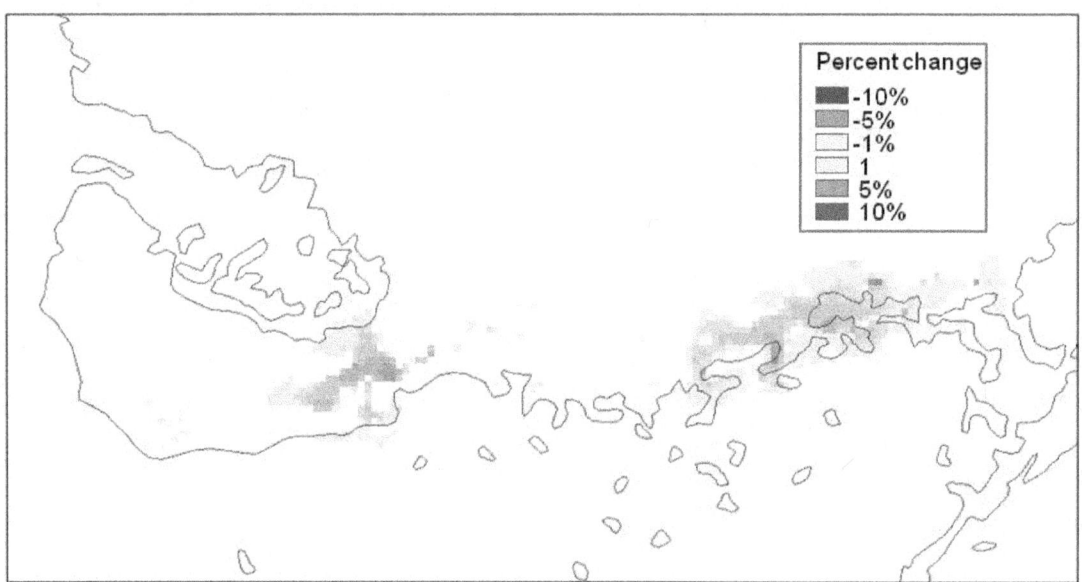

Figure 17. Percent change between hatchling American crocodile density and distribution under CERP0 conditions compared to CERP2050 conditions (Year 80).

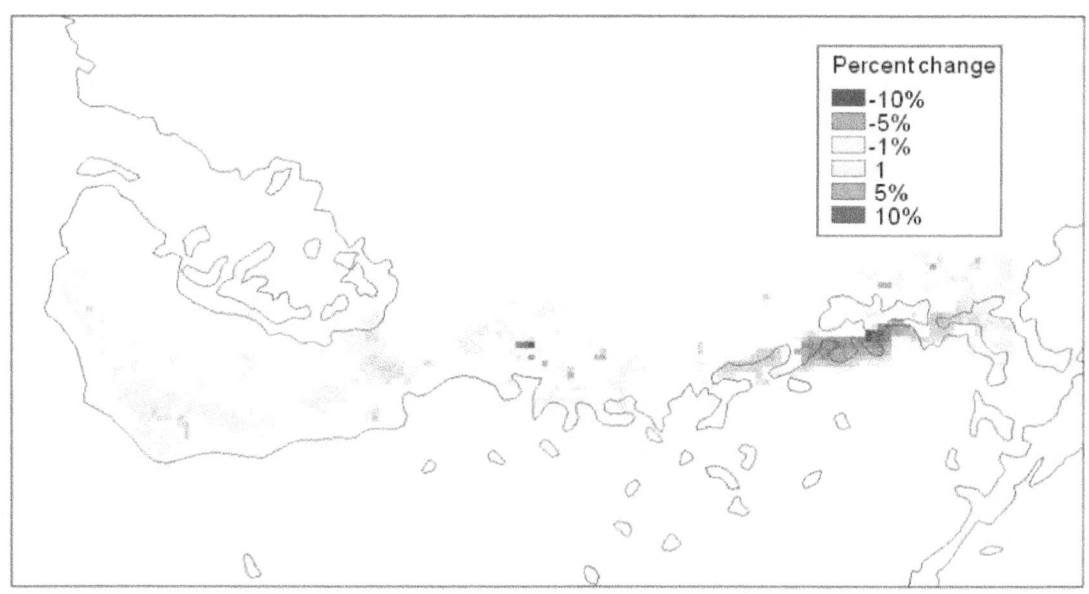

Figure 18. Percent change between hatchling and juvenile American crocodile density and distribution under CERP0 conditions compared to CERP2050 conditions (Year 39).

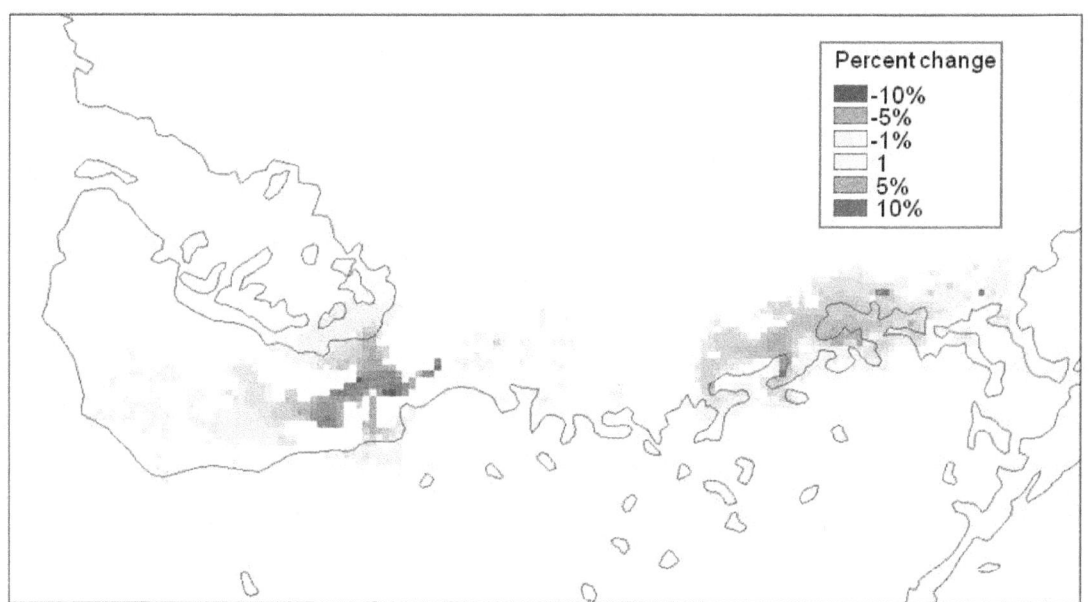

Figure 19. Percent change between hatchling and juvenile American crocodile density and distribution under CERP0 conditions compared to CERP2050 conditions (Year 80)

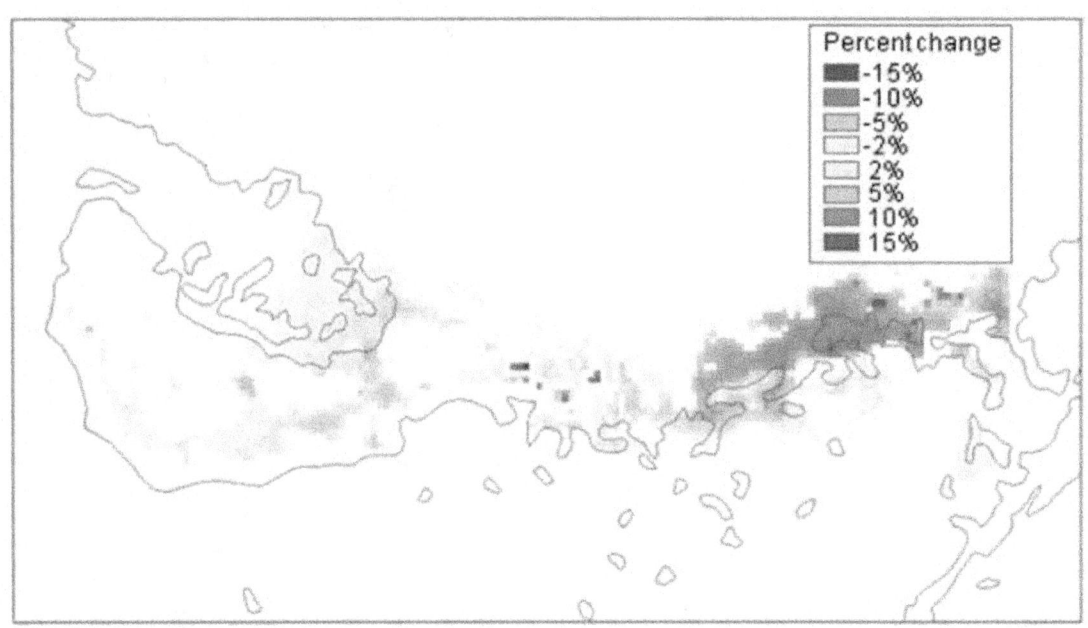

Figure 20.   Percent change between subadult American crocodile density and distribution under CERP0 conditions compared to CERP2050 conditions (Year 39).

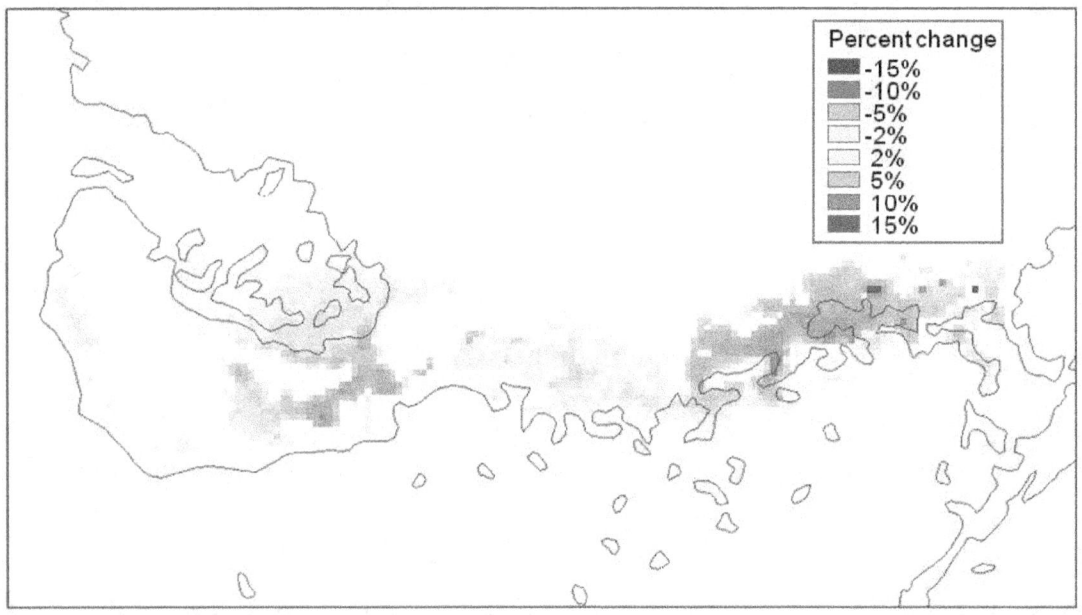

Figure 21.   Percent change between subadult American crocodile density and distribution under CERP0 conditions compared to CERP2050 conditions (Year 80).

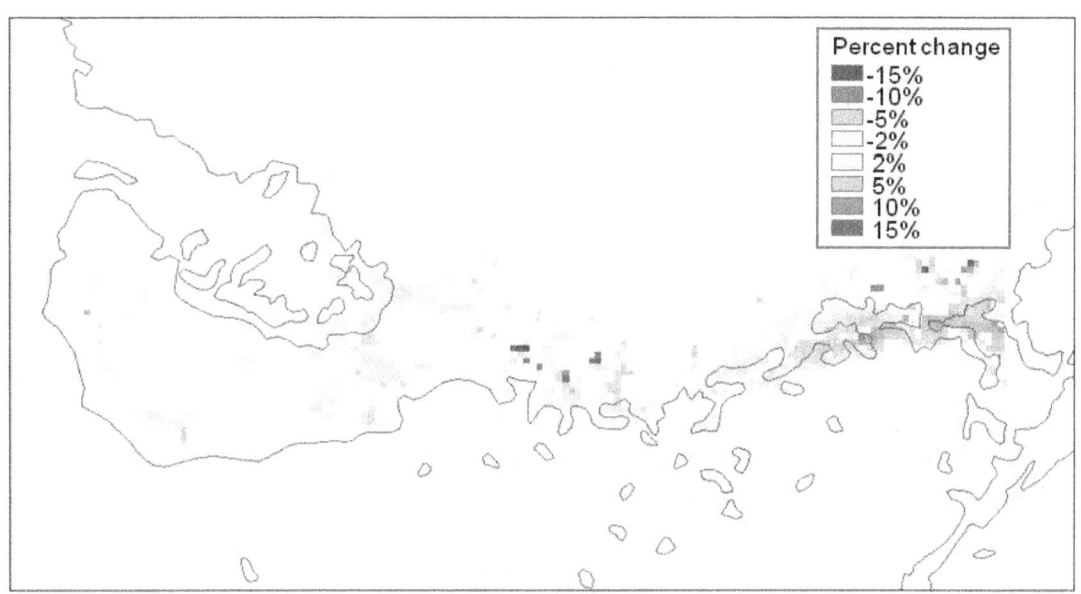

Figure 22. Percent change between adult American crocodile density and distribution under CERP0 conditions compared to CERP2050 conditions (Year 39).

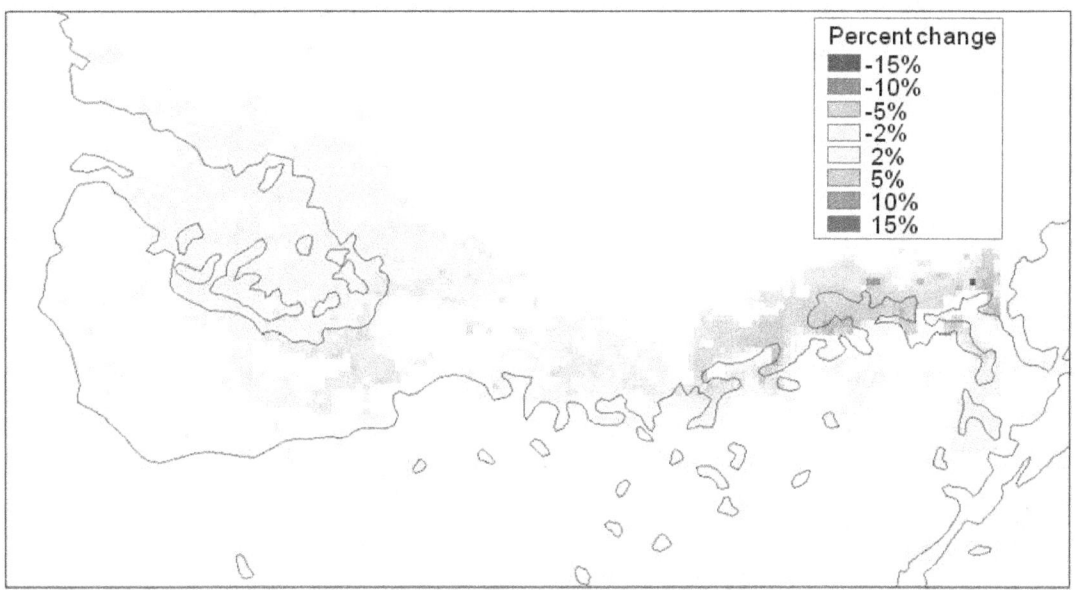

Figure 23. Percent change between adult American crocodile density and distribution under CERP0 conditions compared to CERP2050 conditions (Year 80).

The percent change maps compared crocodile density and distribution under CERP0 and CERP2050 for the hatchling stage, the hatchling and juvenile stages combined, the subadult stage, the adult stage, and all combined crocodile stages. Output from year 39 presented a scenario in which hatchling and juvenile population sizes were the lowest in 100 years of model output, and output from year 80 presented a scenario in which hatchling and juvenile population size was the greatest for 100 years of model output.

Overall, the changes in density and distribution were fairly small and rarely exceeded a 15 percent positive or negative change in density. Hatchling and juvenile changes in percent density did not exceed 10 percent. Adult crocodiles in year 80 were the exception. Adult crocodile density in year 80 increased by 25 percent in some areas of northeastern Florida Bay under CERP0 conditions. Hatchling and juvenile crocodiles appeared to fare better in northeastern Florida Bay under CERP0 conditions in the wetter years and fared better under CERP2050 conditions in the driest years.

Hatchling and juvenile density and distribution fluctuated in northeastern Florida Bay in response to CERP implementation (figs. 24 and 25). Areas exposed to coastal influences, such as Little Madeira Bay and the bays and coves just south of Joe Bay (including Alligator Bay, Davis Cove, and Trout Cove), experienced a slight decrease in crocodile density and distribution at times under CERP implementation. However, interior areas such as Joe Bay and the surrounding inland habitat experienced an increase, or at worst, no change

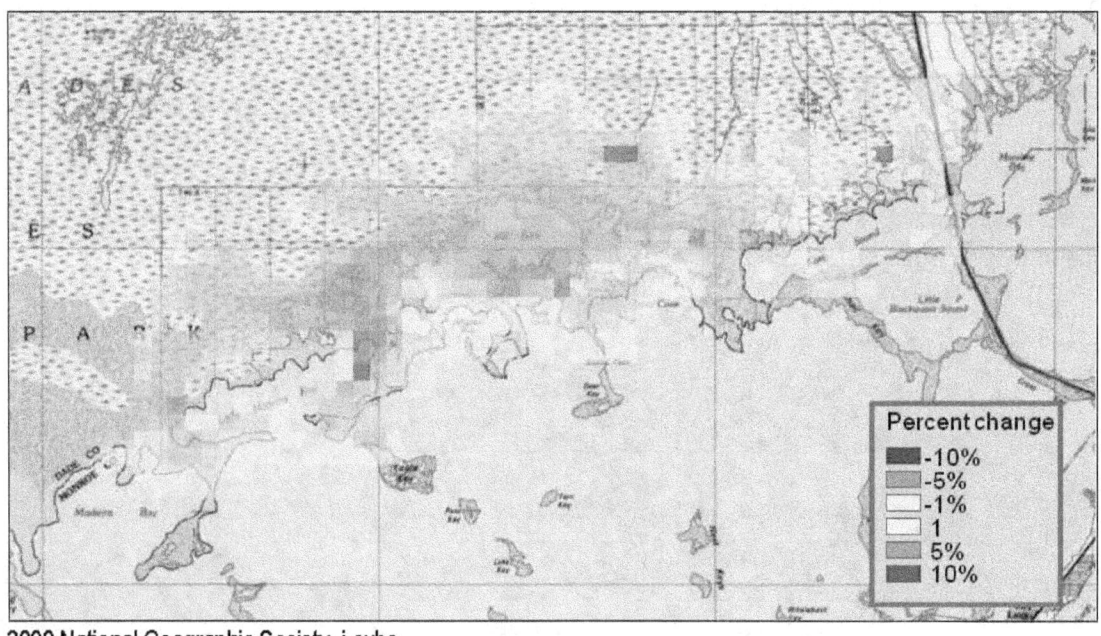

2009 National Geographic Society, i-cube
Web Mercator Auxiliary Sphere (WKID 102100)

Figure 24. Percent change between hatchling and juvenile American crocodile density and distribution under CERP0 conditions compared to CERP2050 conditions in northeastern Florida Bay (Year 39).

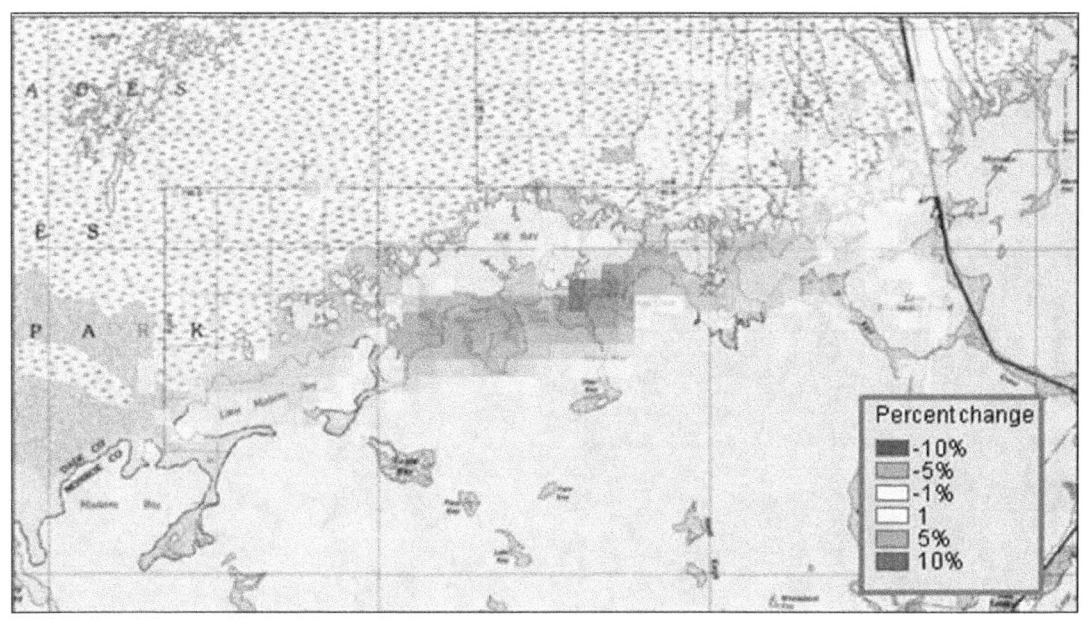

Figure 25. Percent change between hatchling and juvenile American crocodile density and distribution under CERP0 conditions compared to CERP2050 conditions in northeastern Florida Bay (Year 80).

Total crocodile density and distribution (sum of hatchling, juvenile, subadult, and adult stage classes) consistently increased around Joe Bay and Little Madeira Bay in response to CERP restoration regardless of the year (figs. 26 and 27). Hatchlings and juveniles may decline due to the annual variation in precipitation patterns, but over an extended period, it appears CERP restoration will benefit crocodile populations in northeastern Florida Bay.

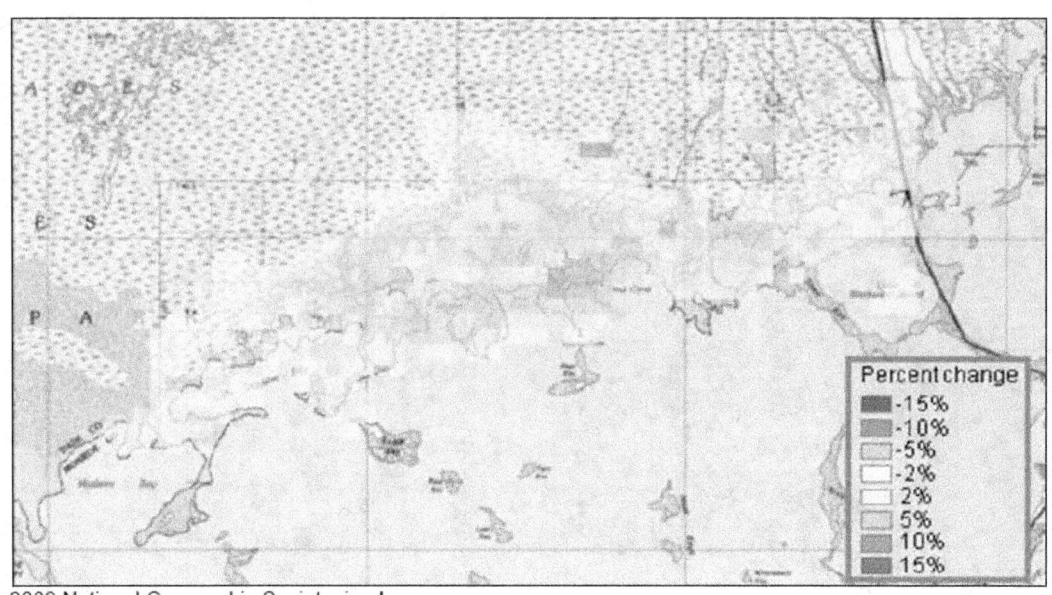

2009 National Geographic Society, i-cube
Web Mercator Auxiliary Sphere (WKID 102100)

Figure 26. Percent change between total American crocodile density and distribution under CERP0 conditions compared to CERP2050 conditions in northeastern Florida Bay (Year 39).

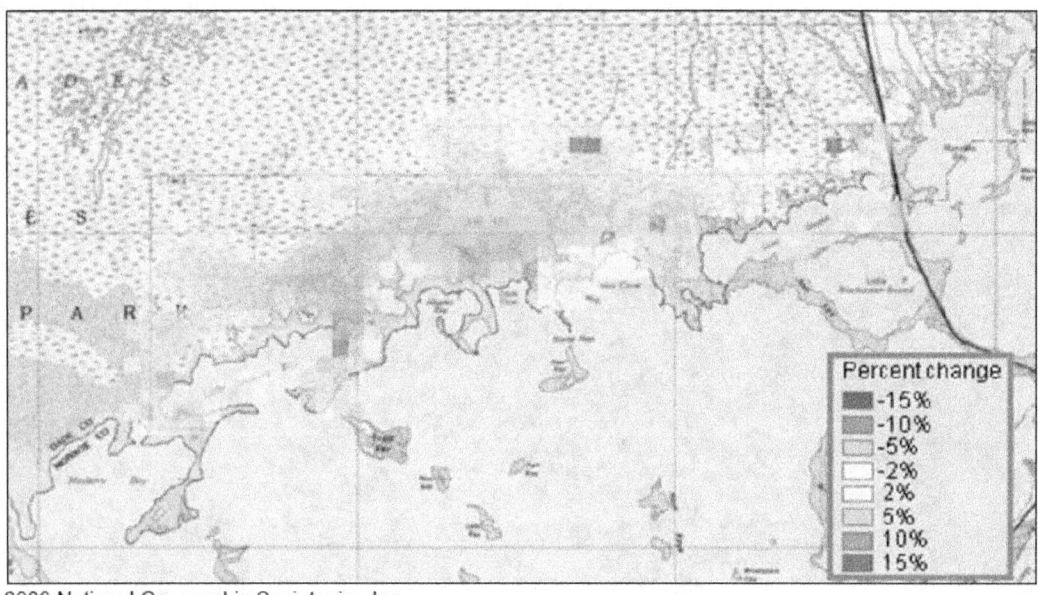

2009 National Geographic Society, i-cube
Web Mercator Auxiliary Sphere (WKID 102100)

Figure 27. Percent change between total American crocodile density and distribution under CERP0 conditions compared to CERP2050 conditions in northeastern Florida Bay (Year 80).

CERP0 conditions generally resulted in a greater crocodile density and distribution in northeastern Florida Bay compared to CERP2050 conditions, and a lower density and distribution for all stage classes of crocodiles around Buttonwood Canal, Coot Bay, Mud Lake, and Bear Lake (figs. 28 and 29). This area has experienced an increase in crocodile density and distribution in recent years. An increase in salinity in this area as a result of CERP restoration efforts would negatively impact the American crocodile population.

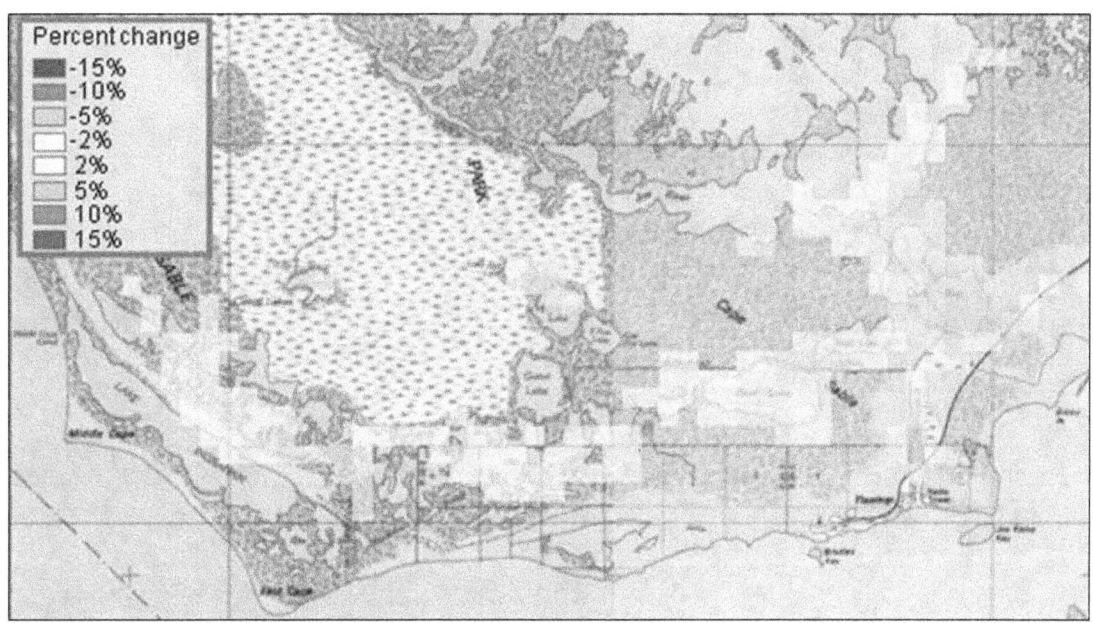

2009 National Geographic Society, i-cube
Web Mercator Auxiliary Sphere (WKID 102100)

Figure 28. Percent change between total American crocodile density and distribution under CERP0 conditions compared to CERP2050 conditions on Cape Sable (Year 39).

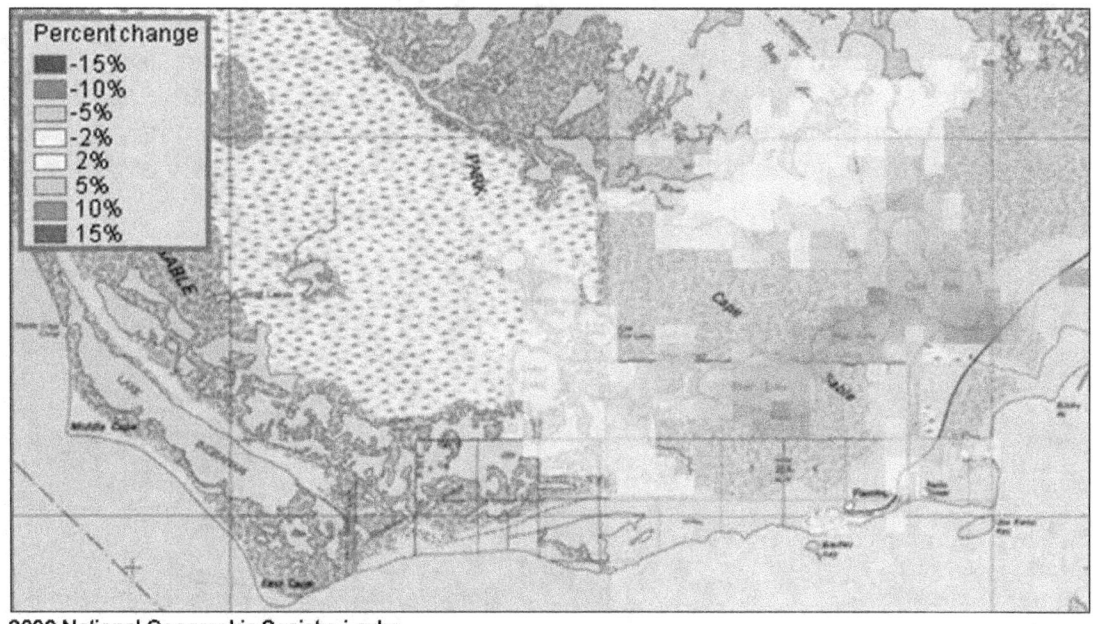

2009 National Geographic Society, i-cube
Web Mercator Auxiliary Sphere (WKID 102100)

Figure 29.   Percent change between total American crocodile density and distribution under CERP0 conditions compared to CERP2050 conditions on Cape Sable (Year 80).

Validation

A qualitative validation of the model was completed using crocodile spotlight data from surveys conducted during 2004-2008. Systematic spotlight data from 1996-2002, which match the calibration dates from the TIME model output, do not exist. Once the TIME model is expanded and calibrated using conditions from 2004-2008, quantitative validation of the model will be possible.

Figure 30 shows the entire spatial extent of potential crocodile habitat within the model boundary. The crocodile model boundary is the same as the TIME model boundary with the addition of areas along the southwestern coast of Cape Sable frequently used by crocodiles, and locations in Florida Bay frequently used by nesting females. Potential crocodile habitat covers a much greater area than that currently inhabited by crocodiles.

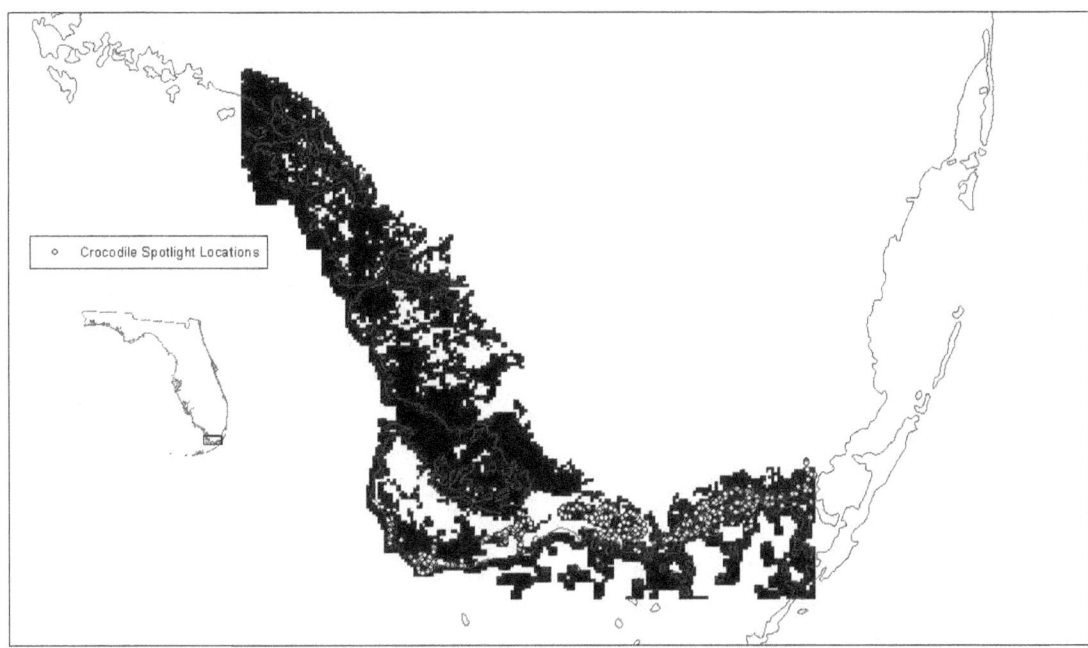

Figure 30. Extent of American crocodile habitat and American crocodile sightings from spotlight survey locations for 2004-2008 within the model boundary.

Figure 31 shows the potential crocodile habitat where crocodiles are frequently observed during spotlight surveys. A large number of hatchling crocodiles, are visible in Buttonwood Canal and largely absent from areas around West Lake.

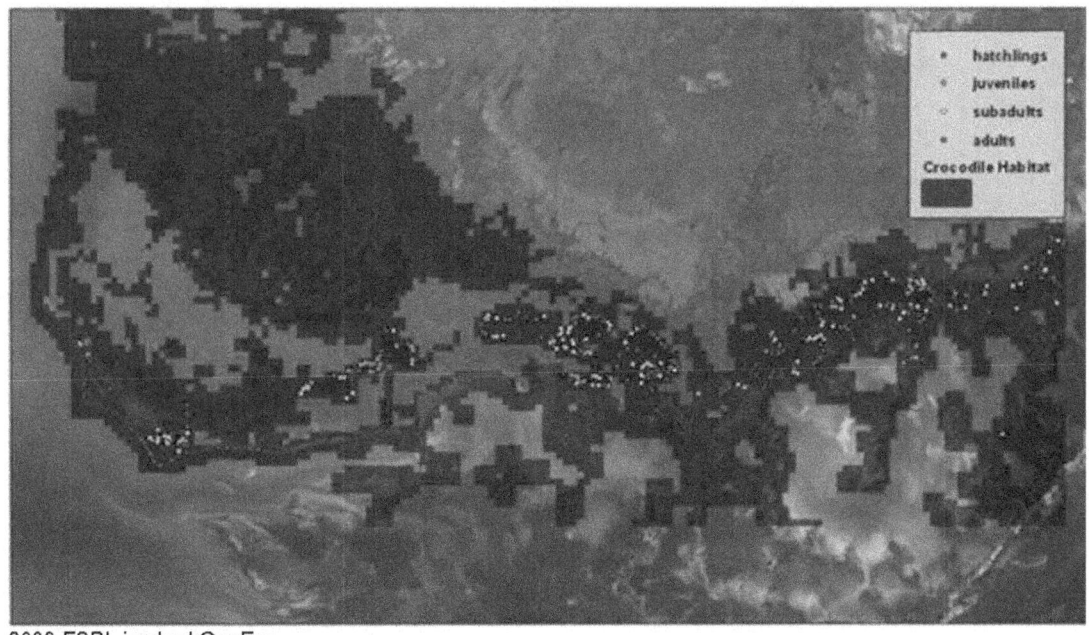

2009 ESRI, i-cubed GeoEye
Web Mercator Auxiliary Sphere (WKID 102100)

Figure 31. American crocodile stage data from spotlight surveys for 2004–2008.

Figure 32 shows the changes in crocodile population size for adults, subadults, and hatchlings and juveniles using the calibrated R158, CERP0 and CERP2050 models for 100 years of crocodile model output. The CERP0 and CERP2050 output indicated a slightly larger population size than the calibrated R158 model output.

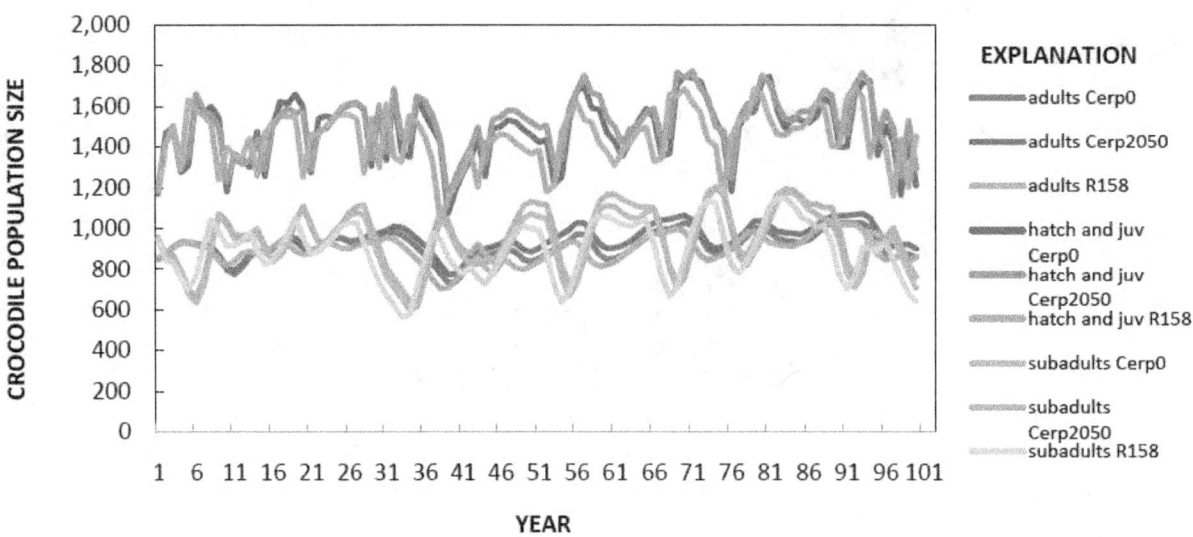

Figure 32. Changes in American crocodile population size by crocodile stage using CERP0, CERP2050, and R158 hydrology model output.

Lacking spotlight data from 1996 to 2000 to validate crocodile density and distribution within the model, the most current spotlight data from 2004 to 2008 were used instead. Years with similar precipitation were matched between the two data sets, and crocodile counts from the matched years were used to qualitatively compare crocodile populations in the model cells with corresponding spotlight surveys. The following figures show model output of crocodile density and distribution using the calibrated R158 model output for hatchlings and juveniles, subadults, and adults (figs. 33-35).

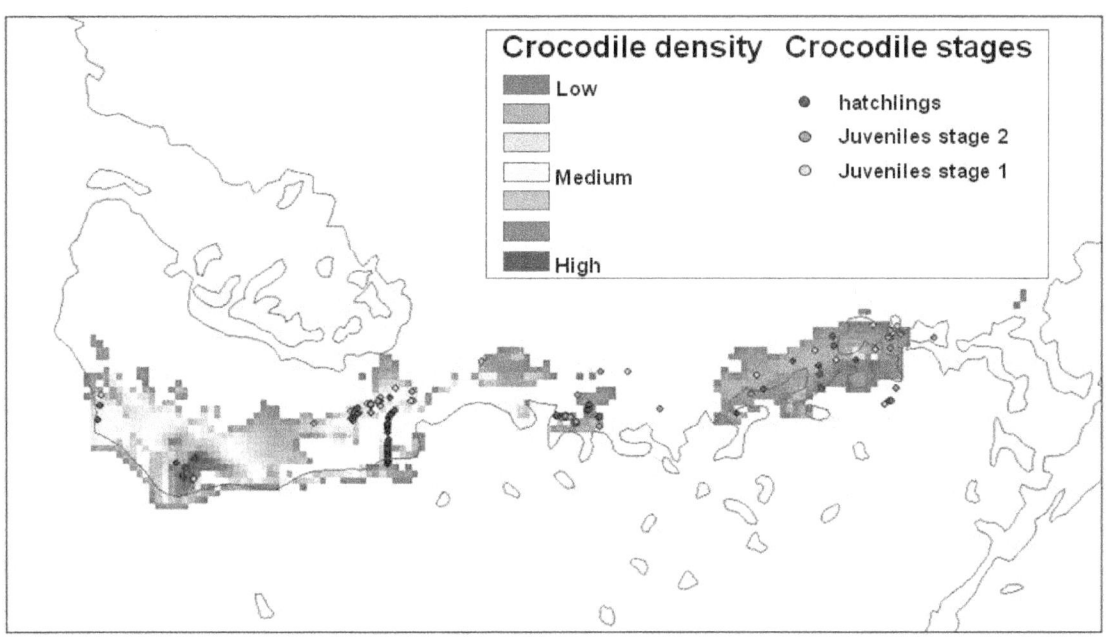

Figure 33. Hatchling and juvenile American crocodile locations from spotlight surveys (2004-2008) compared to calibrated R158 hydrology model output (1996-2000).

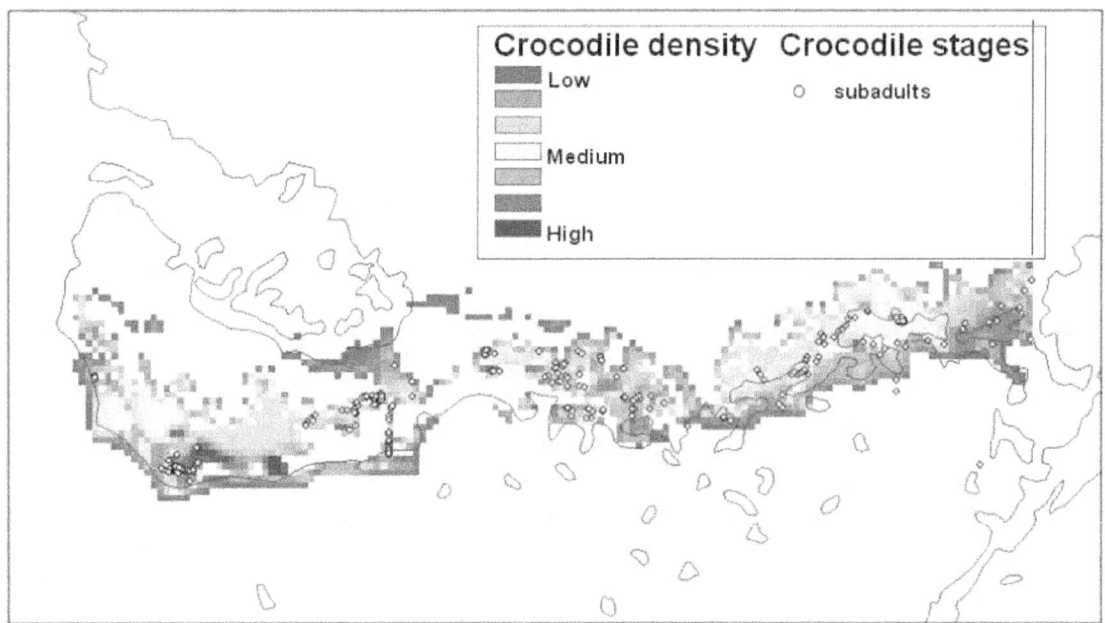

Figure 34. Subadult American crocodile locations from spotlight surveys (2004-2008) compared to calibrated R158 hydrology model output (1996-2000).

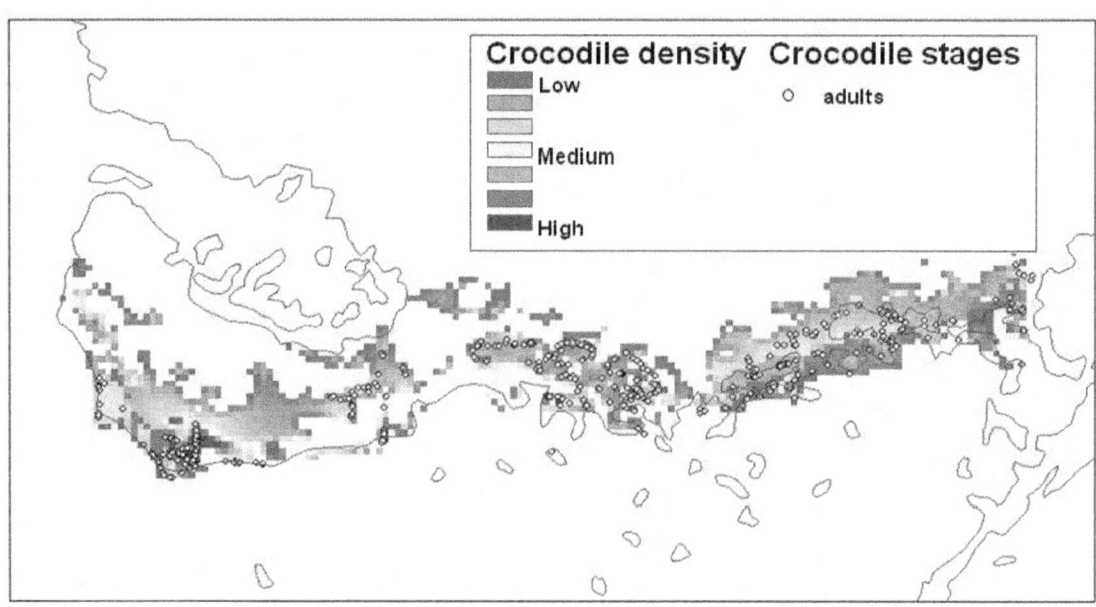

Figure 35. Adult American crocodile locations from spotlight surveys (2004-2008) compared to calibrated R158 hydrology model output (1996-2000).

The qualitative validation showed that crocodile density and distribution for each stage was similar to that observed during spotlight surveys. Four subpopulations with similar density and distribution were observed from the model output and the spotlight surveys for each stage. These subpopulations were most evident in the hatchling and juvenile stage with the greatest densities of young crocodiles being observed on Cape Sable, in and around Buttonwood Canal, in the inland bays south of Cuthbert Lake, and in the protected interior bays of northeastern Florida Bay. As crocodiles mature, they begin to disperse away from nursery habitat. This was seen in the model output as crocodile distribution in the subadult and adult stages spread across the habitat range and into areas not frequented by hatchling and juvenile crocodiles (figs. 33-35).

Discussion

The American crocodile is being used as an indicator to evaluate the impact of potential restoration efforts in areas affected by the Comprehensive Everglades Restoration Plan. Crocodiles were chosen to assess the ecological condition of mangrove estuaries because of their reliance upon estuarine environments characterized by appropriate salinity regimes and adequate freshwater inflows. The desired restoration condition for American crocodiles under CERP is to restore freshwater flow volume and frequency in order to lower salinities in Florida Bay throughout the hatchling period for optimal growth and survival of juvenile crocodiles.

The purpose of developing this spatially explicit crocodile model was to link the most current hydrologic models with crocodile research and monitoring data to gain a better understanding of the potential impact of CERP restoration efforts on the American crocodile population in the Everglades. We were fortunate to be able to use TIME model output from September 2009 for the final output in this report. This recent output included CERP0, a scenario that accounted for all planned changes that would be implemented under CERP restoration, and CERP2050, a scenario that delineated conditions in year 2050 if no system changes were implemented. Throughout much of the active crocodile habitat within the spatial extent of the model, the differences between these two scenarios were minimal, yet there were still observable impacts to crocodile population size, density, and distribution.

The model predicted a fluctuation in population size between years depending upon the different hydrologic conditions produced by fluctuating rainfall. In some years, the CERP implementation resulted in a greater population size, but on average, the overall population size across all crocodile stages was greater without CERP restoration by 2-3 percent. This increase in population size when CERP was not implemented is mostly a result of consistently higher salinities under CERP implementation in areas around Buttonwood Canal, Bear Lake, Mud Lake, and Coot Bay.

The greatest changes in total population sizes appeared to be in response to natural annual variation of precipitation patterns. The greatest decrease in modeled hatchling and juvenile population size was during 1996 when the lowest precipitation on record for the period of CERP model output (1996-2000) was recorded at Royal Palm Ranger Station. These dry conditions resulted in increased salinity concentrations throughout much of northeastern Florida Bay, and had a negative impact on hatchling and juvenile survival rates.

Total crocodile population size across the Everglades was consistently larger across all stage classes when CERP was not implemented, but there were large differences in regional distribution and abundance in response to CERP restoration efforts. Favorable crocodile survival, density, and distribution as a result of CERP restoration efforts were most evident in northeastern Florida Bay. CERP restoration consistently resulted in either an increase in crocodile density or, at worst, no change in crocodile density in the northernmost reaches of northeastern Florida Bay. For most years, CERP implementation resulted in an increase in crocodile density and distribution in northeastern Florida Bay and a decrease in density and distribution of crocodiles around Buttonwood Canal, Coot Bay, Whitewater Bay, and other areas of Cape Sable. Although the positive impact of CERP restoration on historical crocodile habitat such as areas around Joe Bay can be considered a benefit to crocodile growth and survival, the negative impact on Cape Sable populations could overshadow those benefits considering the recent spike in crocodile numbers within this area over the past few years and the projections for future population increases in that area.

Overall, the changes in density and distribution in response to CERP restoration were fairly small and rarely exceeded a 15 percent positive or negative change in density. Additional years of hydrologic model output of CERP alternatives would provide more insight into the costs and benefits of full CERP implementation.

Rainfall

As with all modeling efforts, there are limitations that should be addressed. Hatchling and juvenile growth and survival in relation to salinity were two of the most important driving relationships within the crocodile model. A number of field and laboratory experiments have advanced our understanding of this relationship, yet there are still unknowns. Hatchlings can survive under certain conditions by behavioral osmoregulation (Mazzotti and Dunson, 1984; Mazzotti and others, 1986). Periodic drinking of fresh to brackish water during rain events appears to account for growth of hatchlings in the wild at salinities that are lethal in the laboratory. Relative growth rates may be related to the availability of rainfall in high salinity locations (Dunson, 1982). The capacity of young crocodiles to take advantage of the lens of freshwater that remains on the water surface following a rain event may be an important factor for both growth and survival.

This version of the model did not attempt to model localized precipitation events. The TIME model accounted for precipitation patterns and modeled the flow of freshwater southward through the Everglades but did not account for those localized events that may provide an adequate lens of freshwater at crucial time periods as hatchlings are dispersing toward nursery habitat. Until there is a greater understanding of the relationship between localized rain events and hatchling growth and survival and the ability to model these rain events at an adequately small scale, this model output should be viewed as representing the minimum survival potential. Once this relationship is further understood, the potential exists to incorporate historic and predictive localized weather data into the model.

Conclusions

This spatially explicit stage-based crocodile population model has the ability to predict changes that may occur in crocodile population size, density, and distribution for all ages classes of the American crocodile in response to Comprehensive Everglades Restoration Program alternatives.

Managers will be able to use this tool to better assess the potential positive and negative impacts of restoration alternatives across the greater Everglades for the American crocodile and the mangrove estuaries where they reside. With a spatial resolution of 500 m^2, managers can focus on localized areas to determine whether or not restoration alternatives are expected to have an impact.

This crocodile population model can be efficiently expanded and adapted as CERP restoration goals and efforts continue to evolve. The spatial extent of the FTLOADDS application to the TIME model is already expanding to include areas such as the Ten Thousand Islands and Biscayne Bay. Additional scenarios (such as global climate change) that are expected to have an impact on CERP restoration efforts are already being developed. These expanding spatial extents and climate change scenarios will be incorporated into the crocodile model in the near future.

References Cited

Brandt, L.A., Mazzotti, F.J., Wilcox, J.R., Barker, P.D., Hasty, G.L., and Wasilewski, J., 1995, Status of the American Crocodile (*Crocodylus acutus*) at a power plant site in Florida, USA: Herpetological Natural History, v. 3, p. 29-36.

Cherkiss, M.C., 1999, Status and distribution of the American Crocodile (*Crocodylus acutus*) in Southeastern Florida: Gainesville, University of Florida, unpub. Master's thesis.

Dunson, W.A., 1970, Some aspects of electrolyte and water balance in three estuarine reptiles, the Diamondback Terrapin, American and Salt Water Crocodiles: Comparative Biochemistry and Physiology, v. 32, p. 161-174.

Dunson, W.A., and Mazzotti, F.J., 1989, Salinity as a limiting factor in the distribution of reptiles in Florida Bay: A theory for the estuarine origin of marine snakes and turtles: Bulletin of Marine Science, v. 44, no. 1, p. 229-244.

ESRI, 2008, ArcMap 9.3.

Evans, D.H., and T.M. Ellis., 1977, Sodium balance in the hatchling American Crocodile, *Crocodylus Acutus*: Comparative Biochemistry and Physiology, v. 58, p. 159-162.

Hutton, J., 1989, Movements, home range, dispersal and the separation of size classes in Nile Crocodiles: American Zoologist, v. 29, p. 1033-1049.

Kushlan, J.A., and Mazzotti, F.J., 1989a, Historic and present distribution of the American Crocodile in Florida: Journal of Herpetology, v. 23, p. 1-7.

Lorenz, J.J., 1999, The response of fishes to physiochemical changes in the mangroves of northeast Florida Bay: Estuaries, v. 22, p. 500-517.

Lorenz, J.J., 2000, Impacts of water management on roseate spoonbills and their piscine prey in the coastal wetlands of Florida Bay: Coral Gables, Florida, University of Miami Ph.D. dissertation.

Lorenz, J.J., 2003, Habitat suitability index for roseate spoonbills nesting in northeastern Florida

Bay: Final report for the Cadmus Group prepared by the National Audubon Society.

Lorenz, J.J., McIvor, C.C., Powell, G.V.N., and Frederich, P.C., 1997, A drop net and removable walkway for sampling fishes over wetland surfaces: Wetlands, v. 17, no. 3, p. 346-359.

Mazzotti, F.J., 1983, The ecology of *Crocodylus acutus* in Florida: University Park, Pennsylvania State University unpub. Ph.D. dissertation.

Mazzotti, F.J., 1999, The American crocodile in Florida Bay: Estuaries, v. 22, p. 552-561.

Mazzotti, F.J., Brandt, L.A., Moler, P., and Cherkiss, M.S., 2007, American crocodile (*Crocodylus acutus*) in Florida: Recommendations for endangered species recovery and ecosystem restoration: Journal of Herpetology, v. 41, p. 122-132.

Mazzotti, F.J., Best, G.R., Brandt, L.A., Cherkiss, M.S., Jeffery, B.M., and Rice, K.G., 2009, Alligators and crocodiles as indicators for restoration of Everglades Ecosystems: Ecological Indicators, v. 9S, p. S137-S149.

Mazzotti, F.J., and Cherkiss, M.S., 2003, Status and conservation of the American crocodile in Florida: Recovering an endangered species while restoring an endangered ecosystem: University of Florida, Ft. Lauderdale Research and Education Center Technical Report 2003, 41 p.

Mazzotti, F.J., and Dunson, W.A., 1984, Adaptations of *Crocodylus acutus* and alligator for life in saline water: Comparative Biochemistry and Physiology, v. 79A, no. 4, p. 641-646.

Mazzotti. F.J., and Dunson, W.A., 1989, Osmoregulation in crocodilians: American Zoologist, v. 29, no. 3, p. 903-920.

Mazzotti, F.J., Romañach, S.S., Cherkiss, M.S., Chartier, K.L., Chartier, V., and Brandt, L.A., 2009b, Habitat suitability index model for American crocodiles (*Crocodylus acutus*) in South Florida: Joint Ecosystem Modeling Technical Report DRAFT.

Mathworks, 2008, Matlab, version 7.6.0.324 (R2008a).

Moler, P.E., 1991a, American crocodile population dynamics, final report, study number 753: Tallahassee, Florida, Bureau of Wildlife Research, Florida Game and Fresh Water Fish Commission.

Moler, P.E., 1991b, American crocodile nest survey and monitoring, final report, study number 7533: Tallahassee, Florida: Bureau of Wildlife Research, Florida Game and Fresh Water Fish Commission.

Nichols, J.D., Viehman, L., Chabreck, R.H., and Fenderson, B., 1976, Simulation of a commercially harvested alligator population in Louisiana: Bulletin no. 69: Louisiana State University Agricultural Experiment Station.

Ogden, J.C., 1978, Status and nesting biology of the American Crocodile, *Crocodylus acutus* (Reptilia, Crocodilidae) in Florida: Journal of Herpetology, v. 12, p. 183-196.

Polis, G.A., and Myers, C.A., 1985, A survey of intraspecific predation among reptiles and amphibians: Journal of Herpetological Review, v. 19, no. 1, p. 99-107.

Richards, P.M., 2003, The American Crocodile (*Crocodylus acutus*) in Florida: Conservation Issues and Population Modeling: Coral Gables, Florida, University of Miami Ph.D. dissertation.

Richards, P.M., and Wasilewski, J., 2003, *Crocodylus acutus*: Cannibalism: Herpetological Review v. 34, p. 371.

Schubert, A.W., Mendez, J.H., and Santana, G., 1996, Headstarting and translocation of juvenile Crocodylus acutus in Lago Enriquillo, Dominican Republic, *in* Crocodiles—Proceedings of the 13th Working Meeting of the Crocodile Specialist Group, p. 166-175: IUCN—The World Conservation Union, Gland, Switzerland.

Slone, D.H., Rice, K.G., and Allen, J.C., 2003, Model evaluates influence of Everglades restoration on alligator population (Florida): Ecological Restoration, v. 21, no. 2, p. 141-142

Swain, E.D., Wolfert, M.A., Bales, J.D., and Goodwin, C.R., 2004, Two-dimensional hydrodynamic simulation of surface-water flow and transport to Florida Bay through the Southern Inland and

Coastal Systems (SICS): U.S. Geological Survey Water-Resources Investigations Report 03-4287, 62 p., 6 pls.

Thorbjarnarson, J.F., 1989, Ecology of the American Crocodile, *Crocodylus acutus*, p. 228-258, *in* Crocodiles: Their ecology, management, and conservation: A Special Publication of the Crocodile Specialist Group of the Species Survival Commission of the International Union for Conservation of Nature and Natural Resources.

U.S. Department of the Interior, 2005, Science Plan in Support of Ecosystem Restoration, Preservation, and Protection in South Florida.

U.S. Fish and Wildlife Service, 1999, South Florida Multi-Species Recovery Plan: Atlanta, Ga, 2172 p.

Wang, J.D., Swain, E.D., Wolfert, M.A., Langevin, C.D., James, D.E., and Telis, P.A., 2007: Application of FTLOADDS to simulate flow, salinity, and surface-water Sage in the Southern Everglades, Florida: U.S. Geological Survey Scientific Investigations Report 2007-5010, 114 p.

Appendix 1

Table 1-1. Crocodile model parameters.

Parameter	Acronym	Parameter description	Value	Min.	Max.	Relevant literature
Maxeggs	me	Maximum number of eggs that hatch	39			Mazzotti (2007)
Fecundity	fec	Fecundity vector for the 5 female stages; equivalent to 82% success rate	[.71 .85 1 .85 .67]			Mazzotti (2007)
Hatchsurvinf	his	Influence of daily environmental conditions on hatchling survival	1			Mazzotti and Dunson(1984)
Juvsurvinf	jsi	influence of daily environmental conditions on juvenile survival	1			Mazzotti and Dunson(1984)
Hatchgrowinf	hgi	Influence of daily environmental conditions on hatchling growth	0.6			
Juvgrowinf	jgi	Influence of daily environmental conditions on juvenile growth	0.4			
Subgrowinf	sgi	Influence of daily environmental conditions on subadult growth	0.3			
Femgrowinf	fgi	Influence of daily environmental conditions on female growth	0.1			
Malegrowinf	mgi	Influence of daily environmental conditions on male growth	0.1			
Hatchgrow	hgi	Minimum rate of substage transfer for the hatchling stage	0.508851	1		
Juvgrow	jgi	Minimum rate of substage transfer for the juvenile stage	0.508851	1		
Subgrow	sgi	Minimum rate of substage transfer for the subadult stage	0.53218	1		
Femgrow	fgi	Actual rate of substage transfer for the female stage	0.628957			
Malegrow	mgi	Actual rate of substage transfer for the male stage	0.628957			
Hatchsurv	hs	Hatchlings annual survival rate in the best environmental conditions	0.1			Mazzotti (1991); Moler (1991)
Juvsurv	jsi	Juvenile annual survival rate in the best of environmental conditions	0.7			Moler (1991)
Subsurv	ss	Subadult annual survival rate in the best of environmental conditions	0.85			Moler (1991)
Femsurv	fs	Female annual survival rate in the best of environmental conditions	0.9			Moler (1991); Kushlan and Mazzotti (1989)
Malesurv	ms	Male annual survival rate in the best of environmental conditions	0.9			Moler (1991); Kushlan and Mazzotti (1989)

Appendix 2

Table 2-1. Crocodile model equations.

[ppt, part per thousand; cm, centimeter]

Equation	Description	Range	Minimum	Maximum
	Survival equations			
$S = -0.045(DS) + 1.9$	Influence of salinity on survival and dispersal	20-40 ppt	0.1	1
$C = -0.9 \sum((St5:St8) + (St14:St18) *2) + 1.9$	Influence of crowding on hatchlings and juveniles	1-5 crocodiles	0.1	1
$S_{hatch(t+1)} = S_{hatch(t)} - hsi * (S_{hatch(t)} - S)$	Daily hatchling survival		0.1	1
$S_{juv(t+1)} = S_{juv(t)} - jsi * (S_{juv(t)} - S)$	Daily juvenile survival		0.1	1
$S_{sub} = ones$	Daily juvenile survival			
$S_{fem} = ones$	Daily juvenile survival			
$S_{male} = ones$	Daily juvenile survival			
$St2_{(t+1)} = hatchsurv^{(1/365)} * S_{hatch(t)} * St2_{(t)} * C_{(t)}$	Hatchling population density			
$St3:4_{(t+1)} = juvsurv^{(1/365)} * S_{juv(t)} * St3:4_{(t)} * C_{(t)}$	Juvenile population density			
$St4:8_{(t+1)} = subsurv^{(1/365)} * St4:8_{(t)} * C_{(t)}$	Subadult population density			
$St9:13_{(t+1)} = femsurv^{(1/365)} * St9:13_{(t)}$	Female population density			
$St14:18_{(t+1)} = malesurv^{(1/365)} * St14:18_{(t)}$	Male population density			
	Growth equations			
$Gs_{low} = -0.025(DS) + 1.5$	Influence of salinity on growth during low water	20-40 ppt	0.5	1
$Gs_{high} = -0.025(DS) + 1.25$	Influence of salinity on growth during high water	10-30 ppt	0.5	1
$Gw = -2.084(DM) + 1$	Influence of water depth on growth	0-12.5 cm	0.5	1
$G = Gs_{high/low}^{(1/2)} * Gw^{(1/2)}$	Influence of salinity and depth on growth			
$G_{hatch(t+1)} = G_{hatch(t)} - hgi * (G_{hatch(t)} - G_{(t)})$	Daily hatchling growth			
$G_{juv(t+1)} = G_{juv(t)} - jgi * (G_{juv(t)} - G_{(t)})$	Daily juvenile growth			
$G_{sub(t+1)} = G_{sub(t)} - sgi * (G_{sub(t)} - G_{(t)})$	Daily subadult growth			
$G_{male(t+1)} = G_{male(t)} - mgi * (G_{male(t)} - G_{(t)})$	Daily male growth			
$G_{fem(t+1)} = G_{fem(t)} - fgi * (G_{fem(t)} - G_{(t)})$	Daily female growth			
	Dispersal equations (day 60 - 336)			
$Ds_{low} = -0.025(DS) + 1.5$	Influence of salinity on dispersal during low water	20-40 ppt	0.5	1

Equation	Description	Range	Minimum	Maximum
$Ds_{high} = -0.025(DS) + 1.25$	Influence of salinity on dispersal during high water	10-30 ppt	0.5	1
$Dw = -2.084(DM) + 1$	Influence of depth on dispersal	0-12.5 cm	0.75	1
$D = Ds_{high/low}^{(1/2)} * Gw^{(1/2)}$	Influence of salinity and water depth on dispersal			
circlemap=[sqrt(2),1,sqrt(2);1,1,1;sqrt(2),1,sqrt(2)]	Dispersal kernel foundation	3 x 3 matrix	1	1.4142
$K_{hatch} = D_{hatch} / circlemap$	Hatchling kernel			
$K_{juv} = D_{juv} / circlemap$	Juvenile kernel			
$K_{sub} = D_{sub} / circlemap$	Subadult kernel			
$K_{male} = D_{male} / circlemap$	Male kernel			
$K_{fem} = D_{fem} / circlemap$	Female kernel			
$K_{fem} = dn10k / circlemap$	Female nesting kernel			
$K_{hatch}(2,2) = K_{hatch}(2,2) * 1$	Rate of hatchling dispersal	1		
$K_{juv}(2,2) = K_{juv}(2,2) * 10$	Rate of juvenile stage 1 dispersal	10		
$K_{sub}(2,2) = K_{sub}(2,2) * 1$	Rate of subadult and stage 2 juvenile dispersal	1		
$K_{adult}(2,2) = K_{adult}(2,2) * 5$	Rate of adult dispersal	5		
$K_{fem}(2,2) = K_{fem}(2,2) * 1$	Rate of female dispersal	1		
$St2_{(t+1)} = St2_{(t)} * K_{hatch}$	Hatchling population density			
$St3:4_{(t+1)} = St3:4_{(t)} * K_{juv}$	Juvenile population density			
$St5:8_{(t+1)} = St5:8_{(t)} * K_{sub}$	Subadult population density			
$St9:13_{(t+1)} = St9:13_{(t)} * K_{fem}$	Female population density			
$St14:18_{(t+1)} = St14:18_{(t)} * K_{male}$	Male population density			
$G_{hatch(t+1)} = G_{hatch(t)} * K_{hatch}$			0	1
$G_{juv(t+1)} = G_{juv(t)} * K_{juv}$			0	1
$G_{sub(t+1)} = G_{sub(t)} * K_{sub}$			0	1
$G_{fem(t+1)} = G_{fem(t)} * K_{fem}$			0	1
$G_{male(t+1)} = G_{male(t)} * K_{male}$			0	1

Reproduction and stage transfer equations (day 218)	
$T_{hatch} = ((1 - hg) * G_{hatch} + hg$	Hatchling transfer
$T_{juv} = ((1 - jg) * G_{juv} + jg$	Juvenile transfer
$T_{sub} = ((1 - sg) * G_{sub} + sg$	Subadult transfer
$T_{fem} = fg$	Female transfer

41

Equation	Description	Range	Minimum	Maximum
$T_{male} = mg$	Male transfer			
$St15:18_{(t+1)} = St14:18_{(t)} - (St14:18_{(t)} * T_{male}) + (St14:18 - 1_{(t)} * T_{male})$	Male stages (excluding the first one)			
$St14_{(t+1)} = St14_{(t)} - (St14_{(t)} * T_{male}) + (0.5 * St8_{(t)} * T_{sub})$	First male stage			
$St10:14_{(t+1)} = St10:14_{(t)} - (St10:14_{(t)} * T_{fem}) + (St10:14 - 1_{(t)} * T_{fem})$	Female stages (excluding the first one)			
$St9_{(t+1)} = St9_{(t)} - (St9_{(t)} * T_{fem}) + (0.5 * St8_{(t)} * T_{sub})$	First female stage			
$St6:9_{(t+1)} = St6:9_{(t)} - (St6:9_{(t)} * T_{sub}) + (St6:9 - 1_{(t)} * T_{sub})$	Subadult stages (excluding the first one)			
$St5_{(t+1)} = St5_{(t)} - (St5_{(t)} * T_{sub}) + (St4_{(t)} * T_{juv})$	First subadult stage			
$St4_{(t+1)} = St4_{(t)} - (St4_{(t)} * T_{juv}) + (St3_{(t)} * T_{juv})$	Final juvenile stage			
$St3_{(t+1)} = St3_{(t)} - (St3_{(t)} * T_{juv}) + (St2_{(t)} * T_{hatch})$	First juvenile stage			
$St2_{(t+1)} = St2_{(t)} - (St2_{(t)} * T_{hatch}) + St1_{(t)}$	Hatchling stage			
$eggmap(1:5) = hns * \sum(St9:13) * me * fc(St9:13) * G_{fem}$	Egg map			
$St2 = \sum(eggmap)$				

Hatchling transfer equations (early jump to juvenile stage on day 335)

Equation	Description	Range	Minimum	Maximum
$St3_{(t+1)} = St3_{(t)} + (St2 * T_{hatch})$	Juvenile (stage 1) population density			
$St2 = St2 - (St2 * T_{hatch})$	Hatchling population density			

Appendix 3

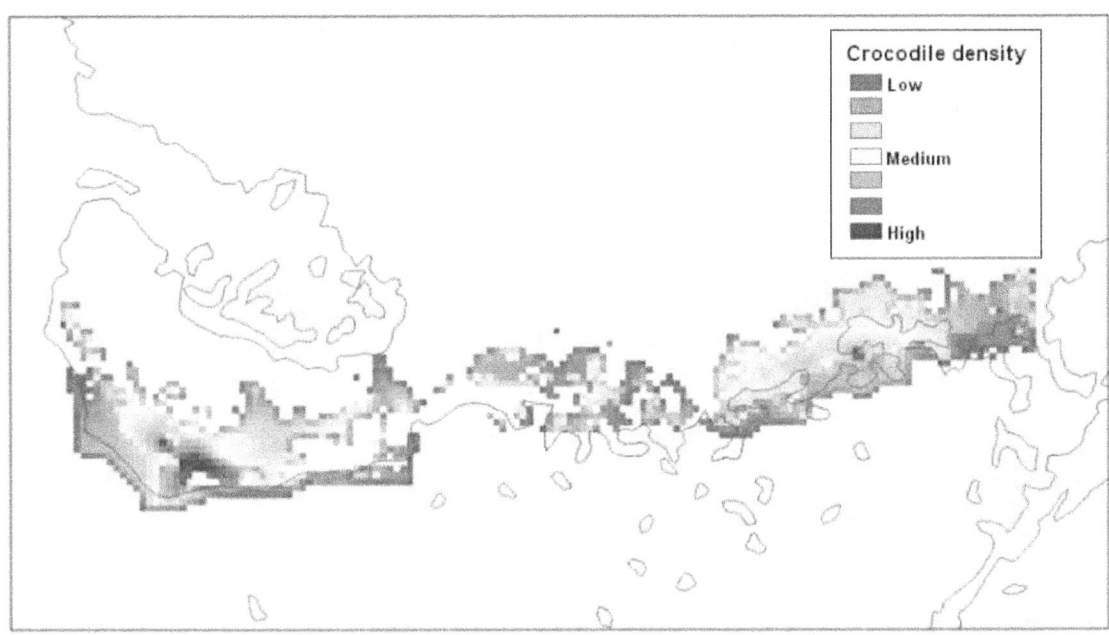

Figure 3-1. American crocodile density and distribution under CERP0 conditions (Year 39).

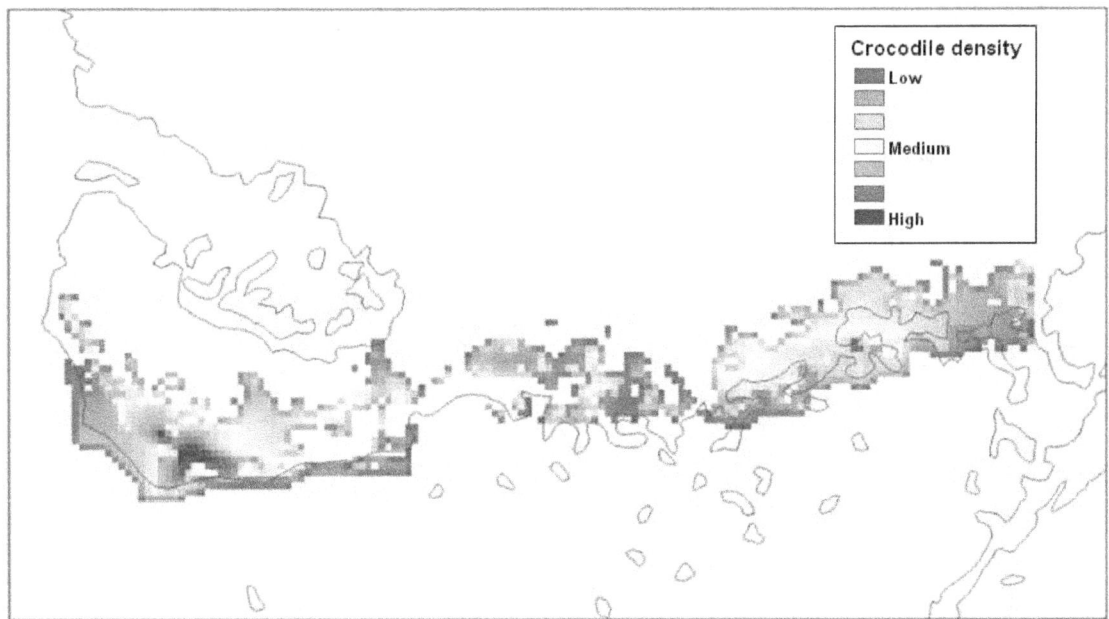

Figure 3-2. American crocodile density and distribution under CERP2050 conditions (Year 39).

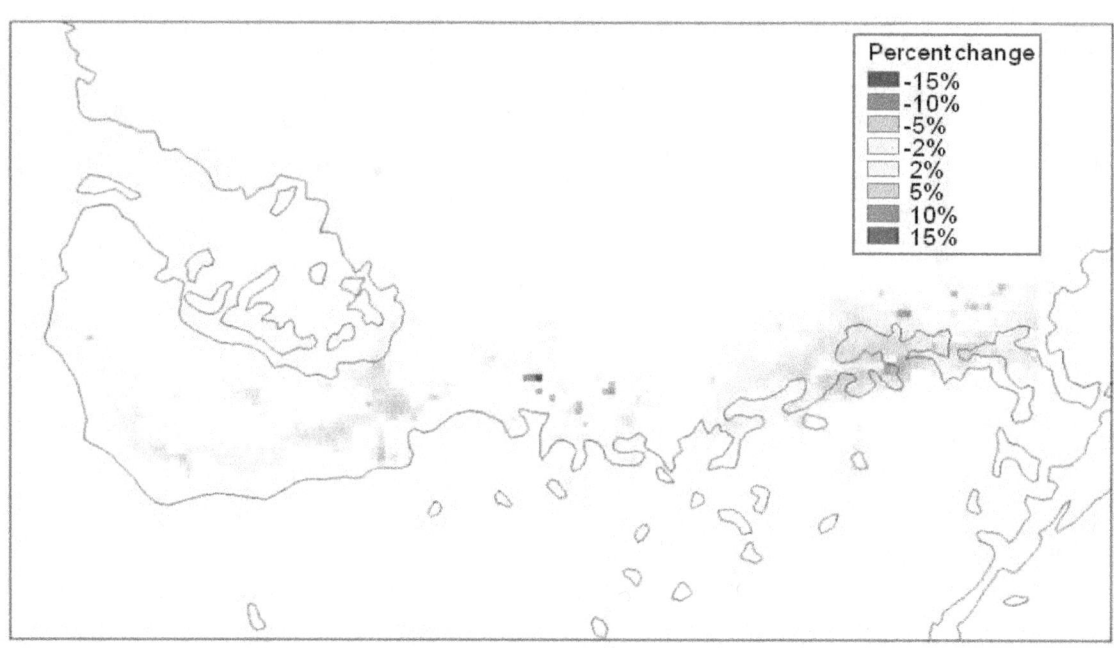

Figure 3-3. Percent change between American crocodile density and distribution under CERP0 conditions compared to CERP2050 conditions (Year 39).

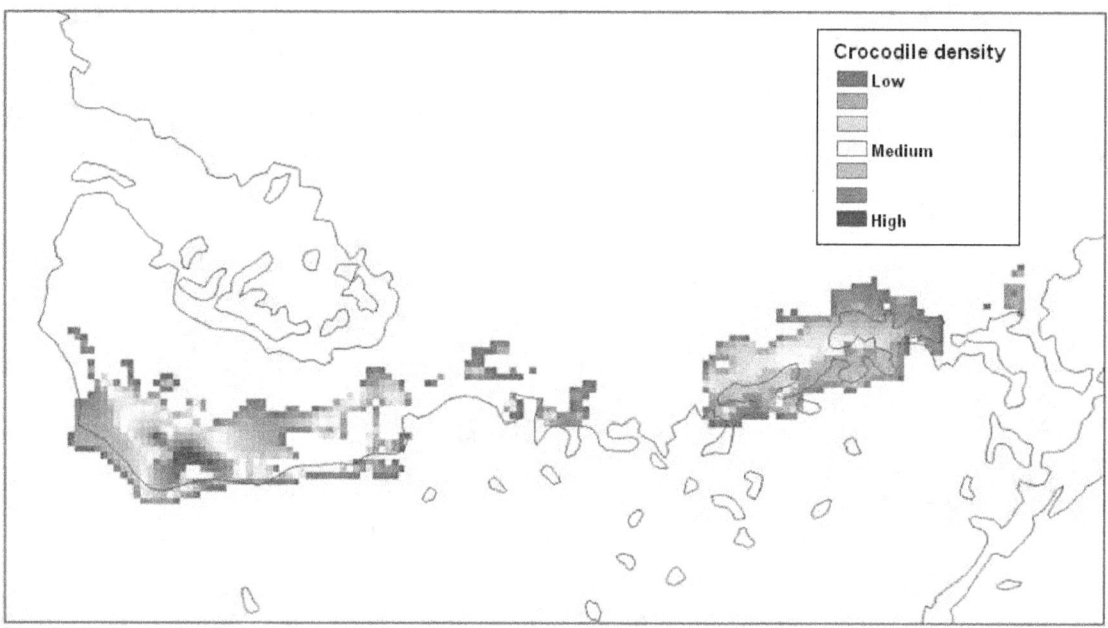

Figure 3-4. Hatchling American crocodile density and distribution under CERP0 conditions (Year 39).

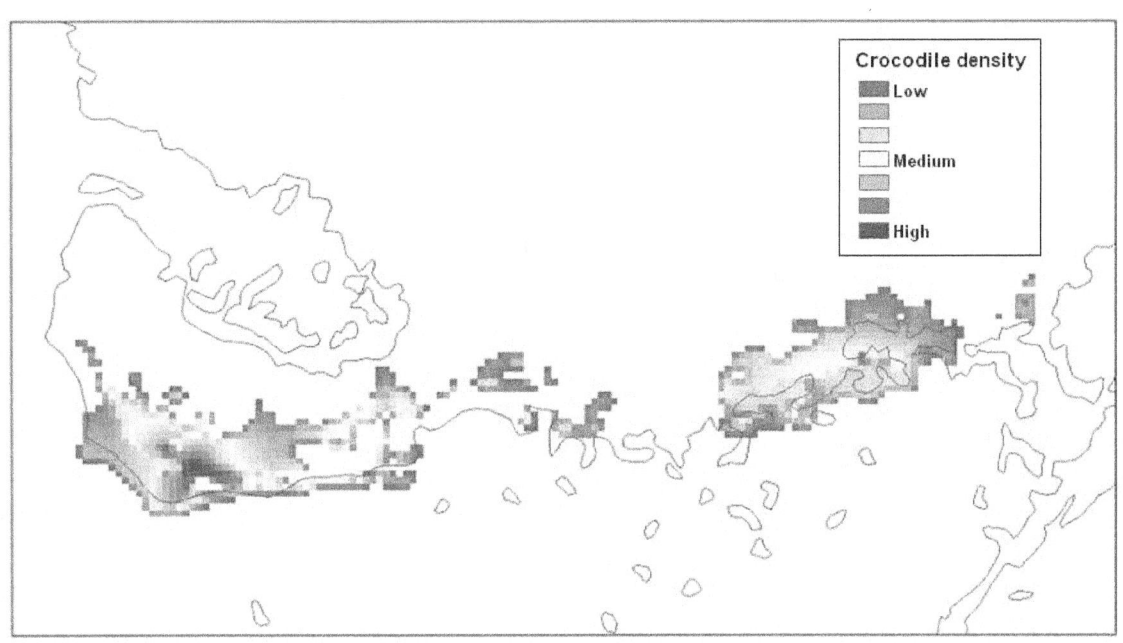

Figure 3-5. Hatchling American crocodile density and distribution under CERP2050 conditions (Year 39).

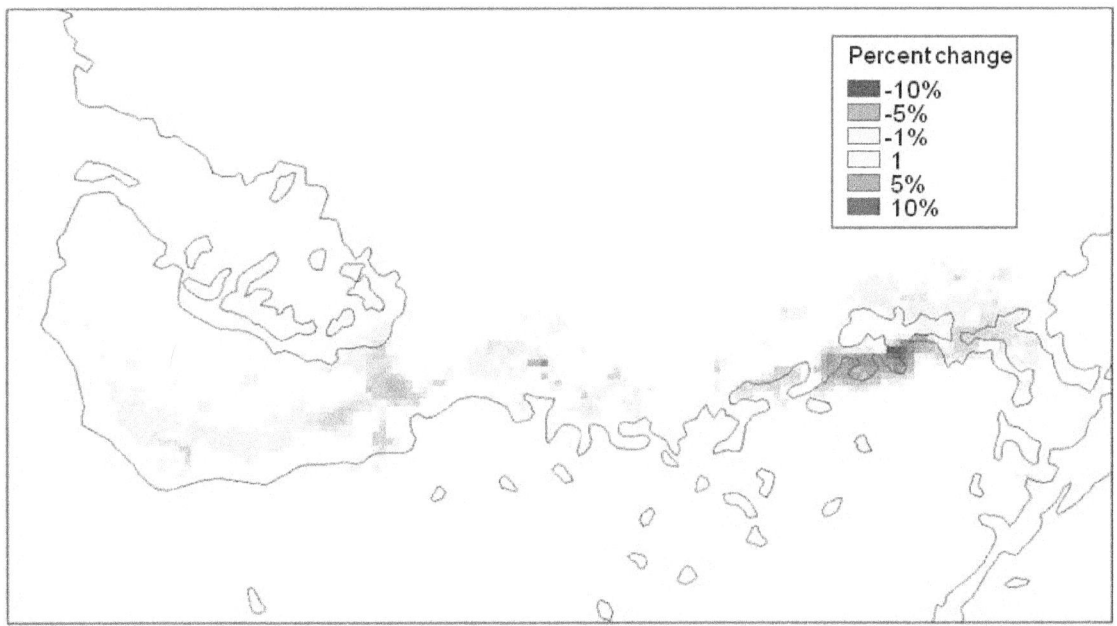

Figure 3-6. Percent change between hatchling American crocodile density and distribution under CERP0 conditions compared to CERP2050 conditions (Year 39).

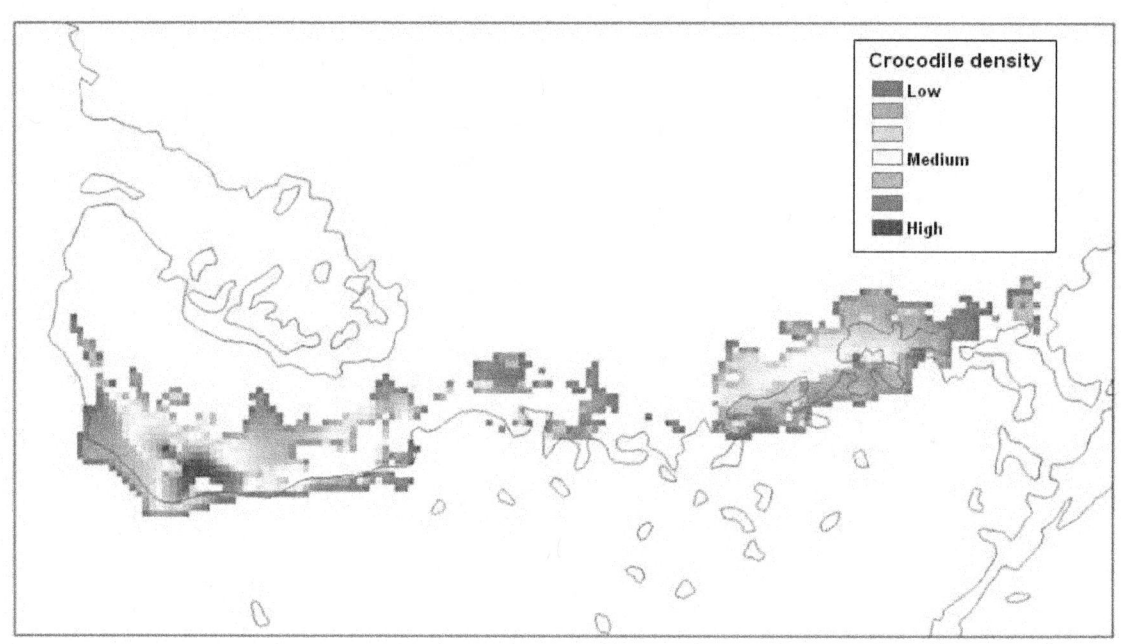

Figure 3-7. Hatchling and juvenile American crocodile density and distribution under CERP0 conditions (Year 39).

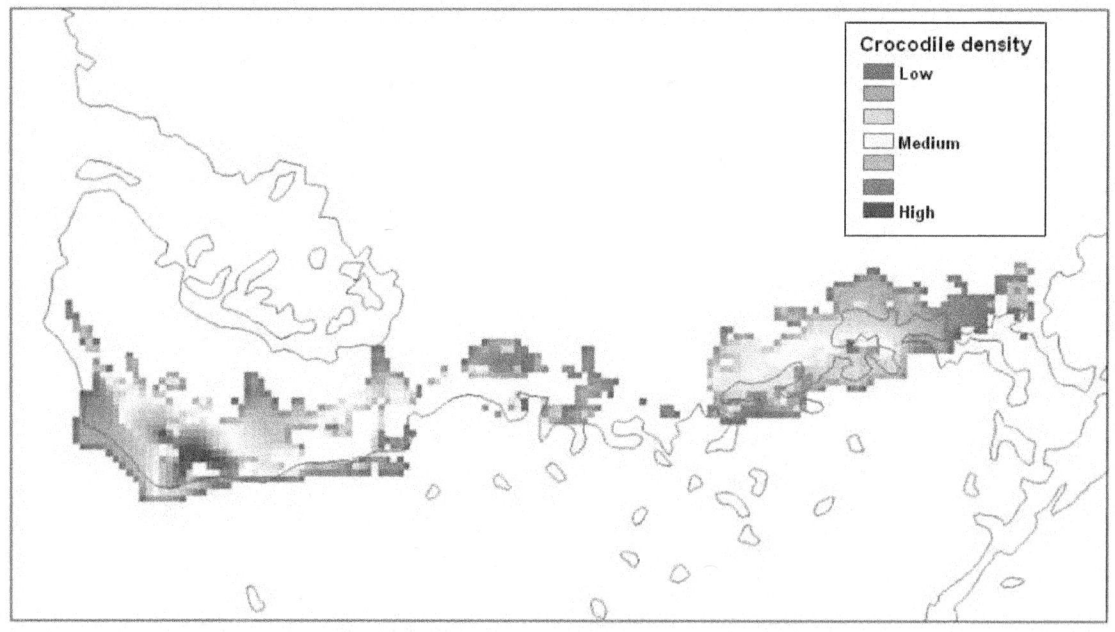

Figure 3-8. Hatchling and juvenile American crocodile density and distribution under CERP2050 conditions (Year 39).

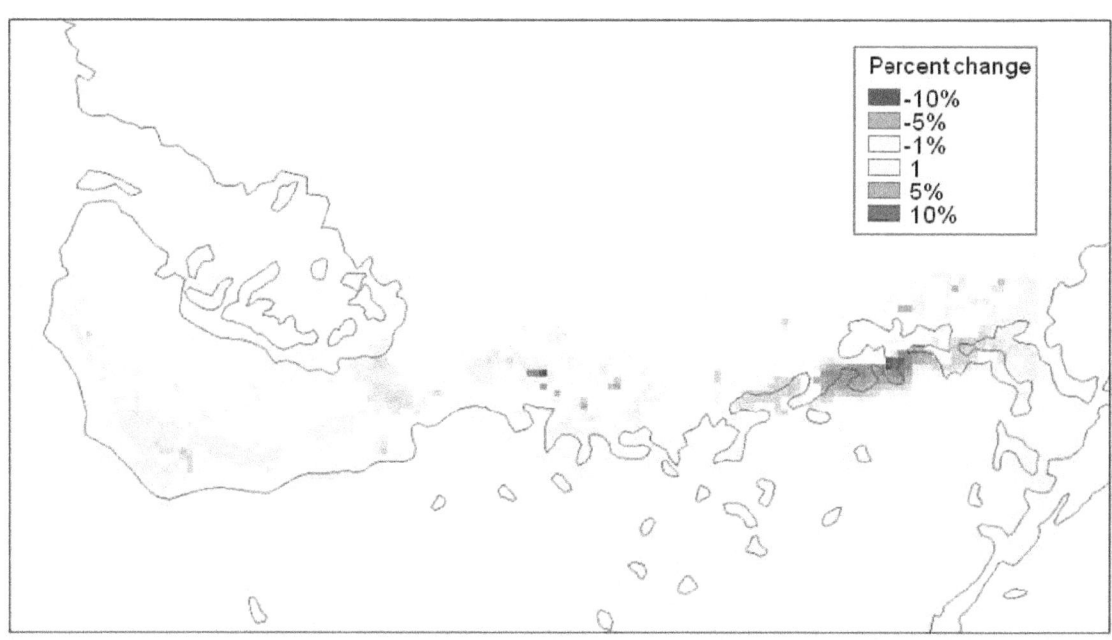

Figure 3-9. Percent change between hatchling and juvenile American crocodile density and distribution under CERP0 conditions compared to CERP2050 conditions (Year 39).

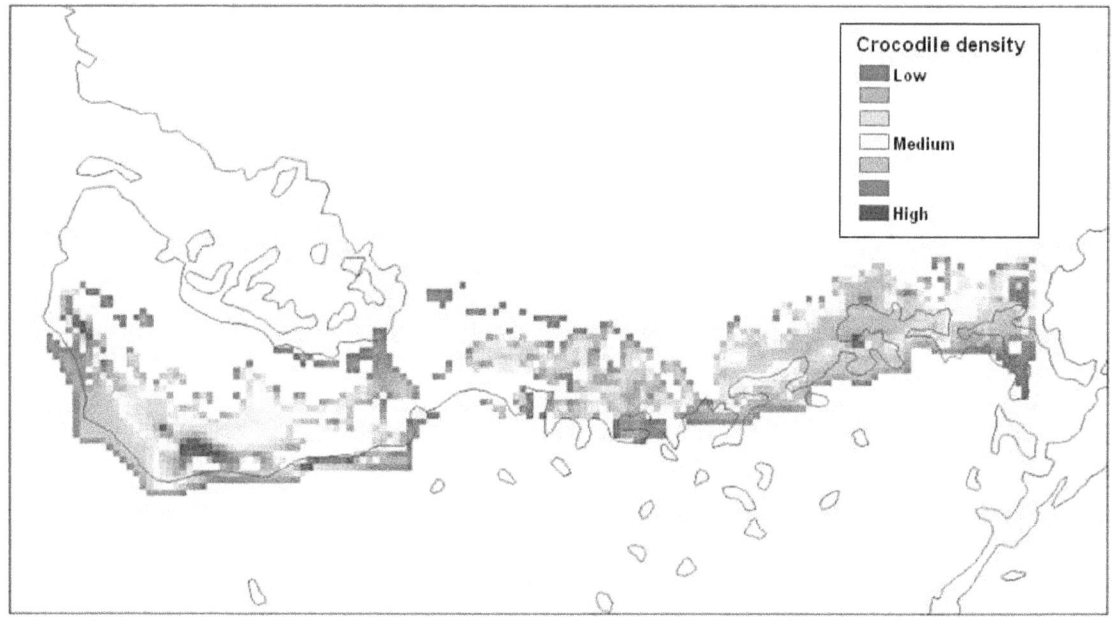

Figure 3-10. Subadult American crocodile density and distribution under CERP0 conditions (Year 39).

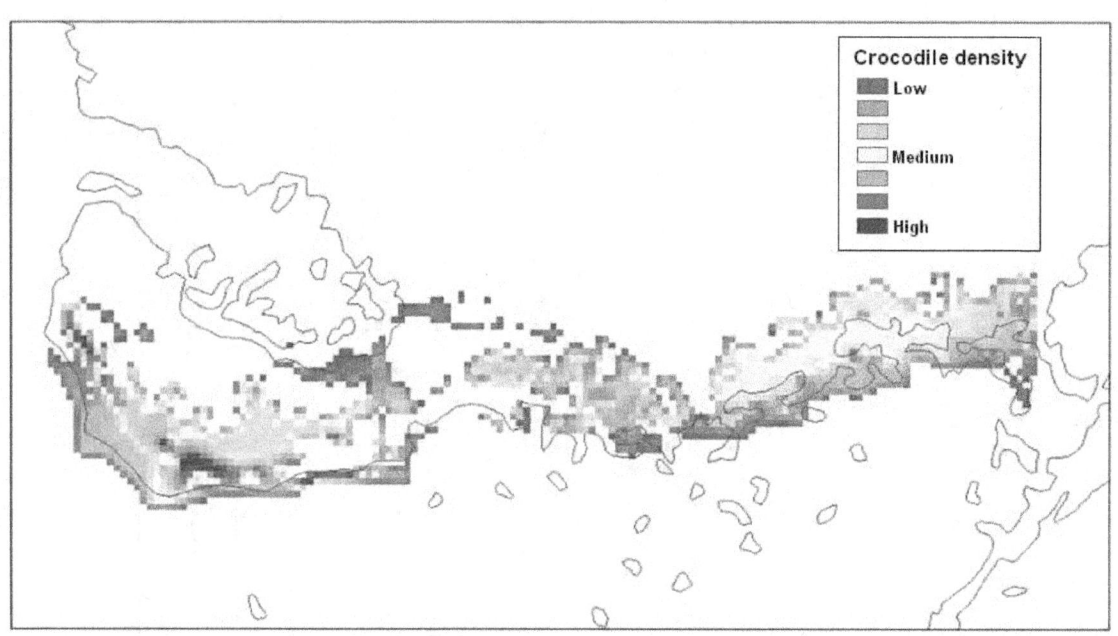

Figure 3-11. Subadult American crocodile density and distribution under CERP2050 conditions (Year 39).

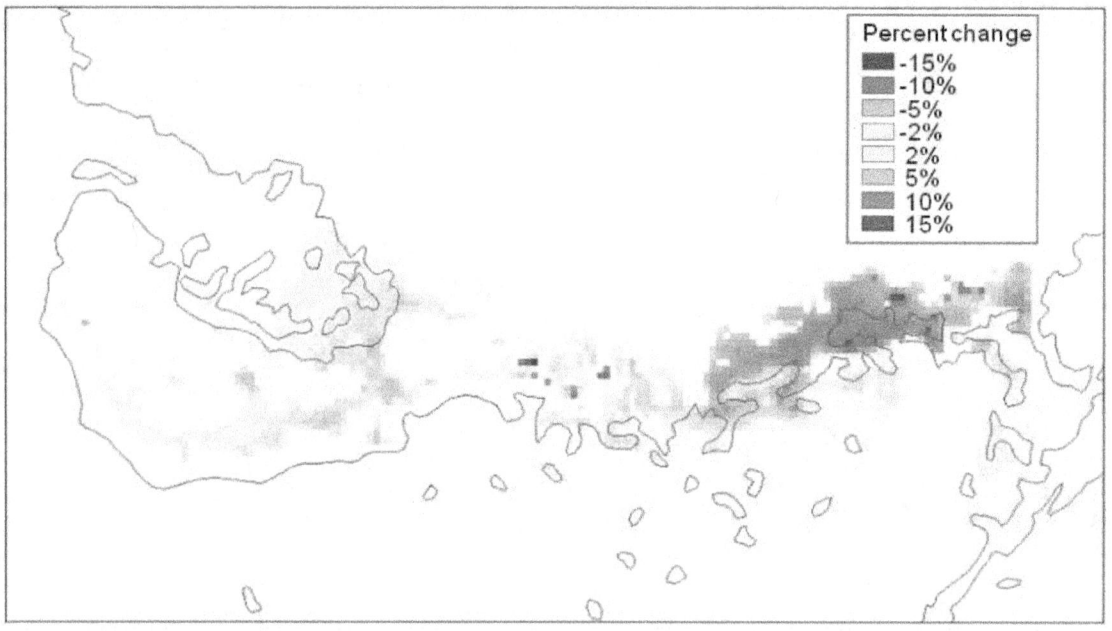

Figure 3-12. Percent change between subadult American crocodile density and distribution under CERP0 conditions compared to CERP2050 conditions (Year 39).

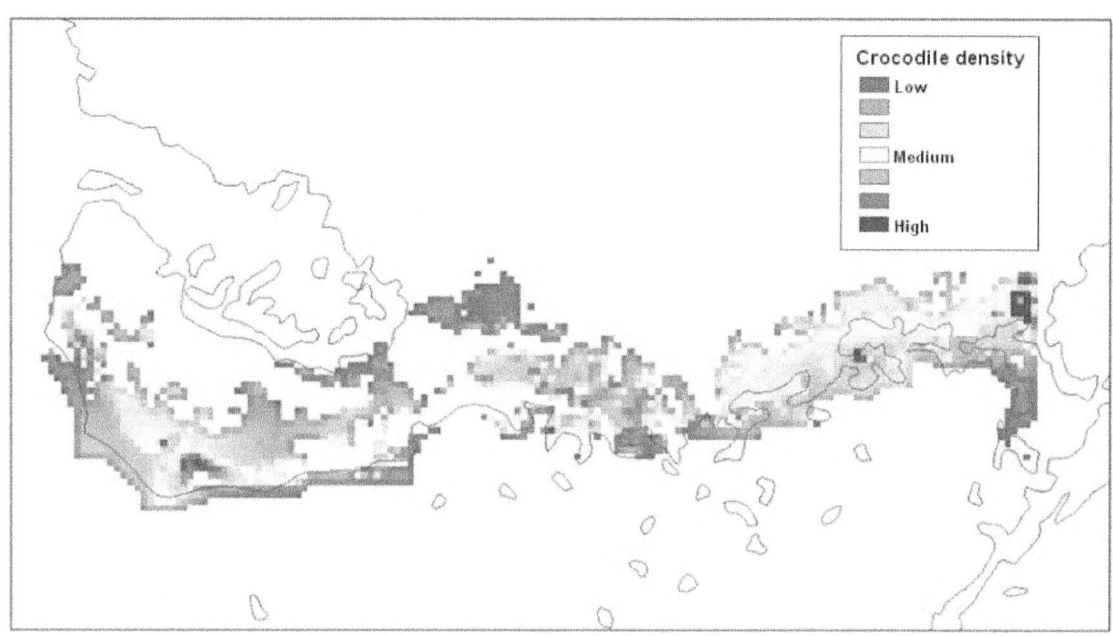

Figure 3-13. Adult American crocodile density and distribution under CERP0 conditions (Year 39).

Figure 3-14. Adult American crocodile density and distribution under CERP2050 conditions (Year 39).

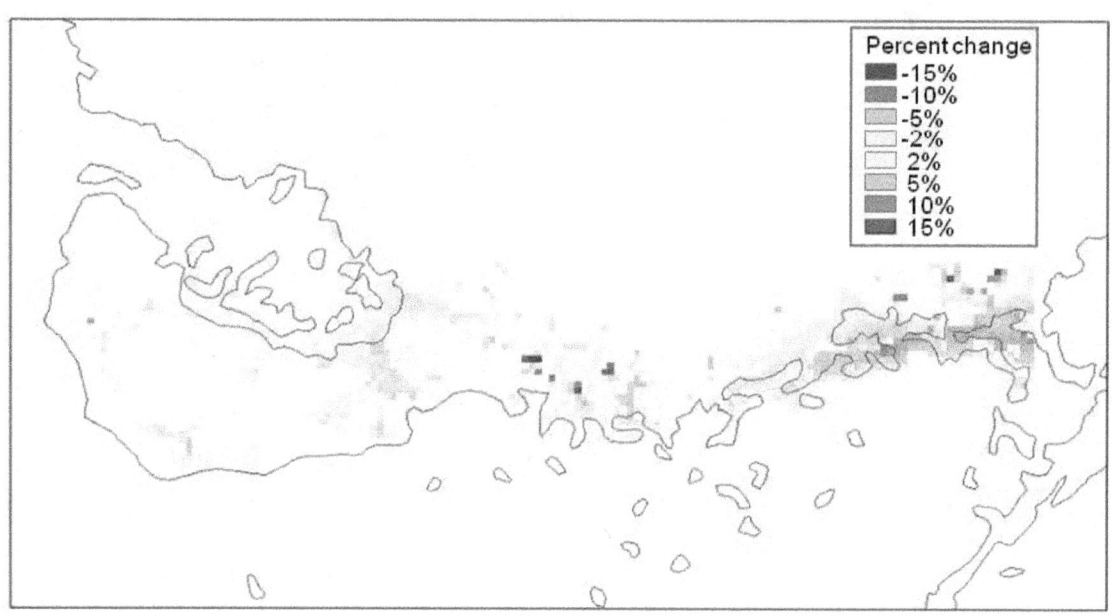

Figure 3-15. Percent change between adult American crocodile density and distribution under CERP0 conditions compared to CERP2050 conditions (Year 39).

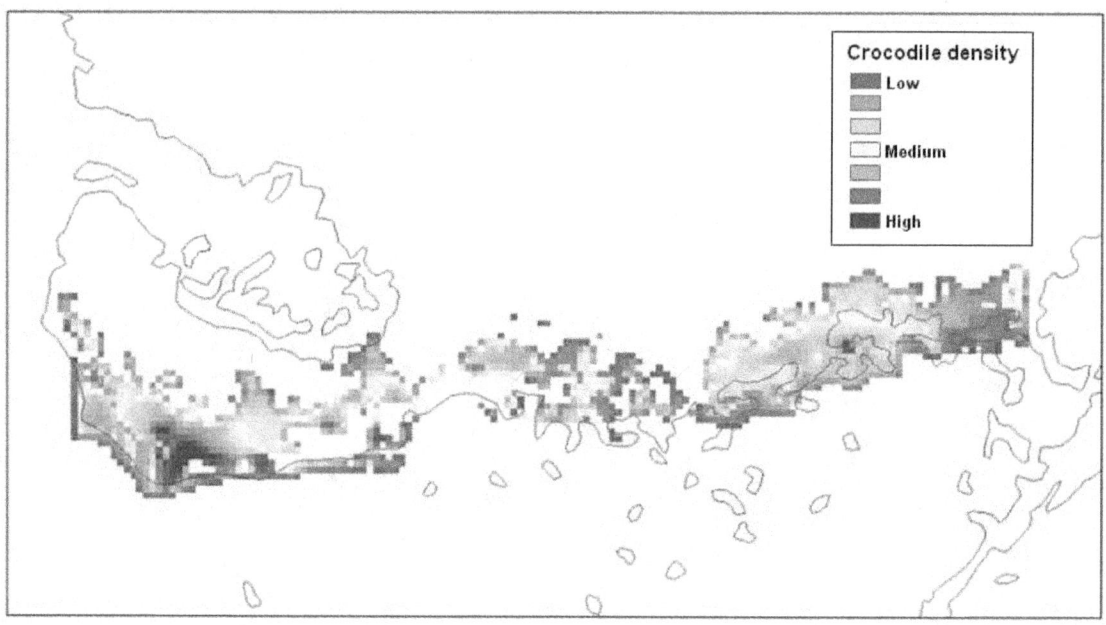

Figure 3-16. American crocodile density and distribution under CERP0 conditions (Year 80).

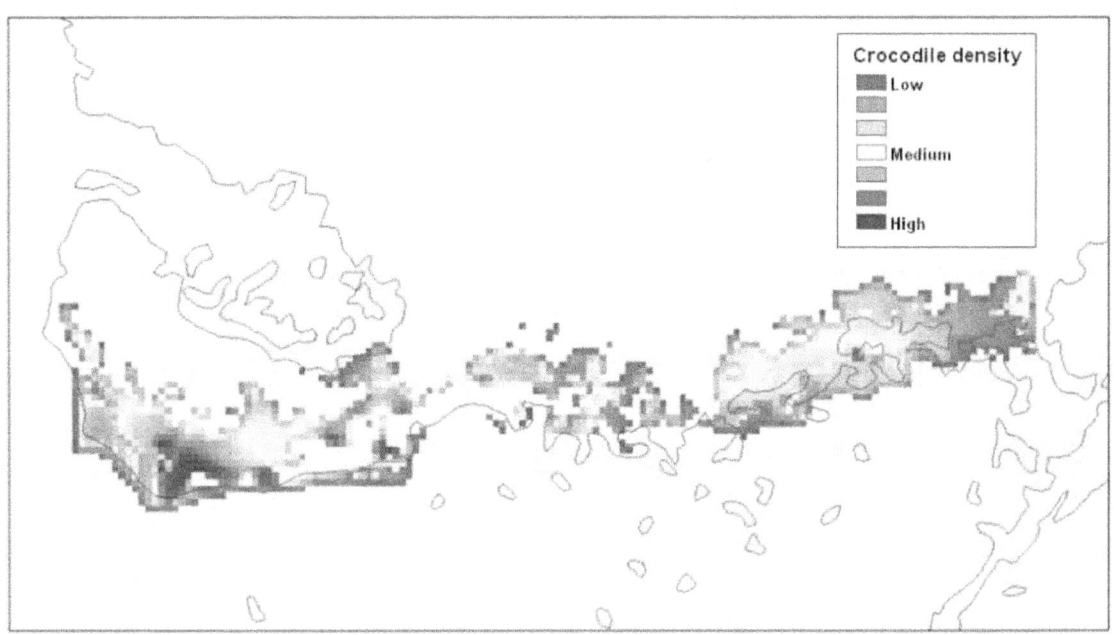

Figure 3-17. American crocodile density and distribution under CERP2050 conditions (Year 80).

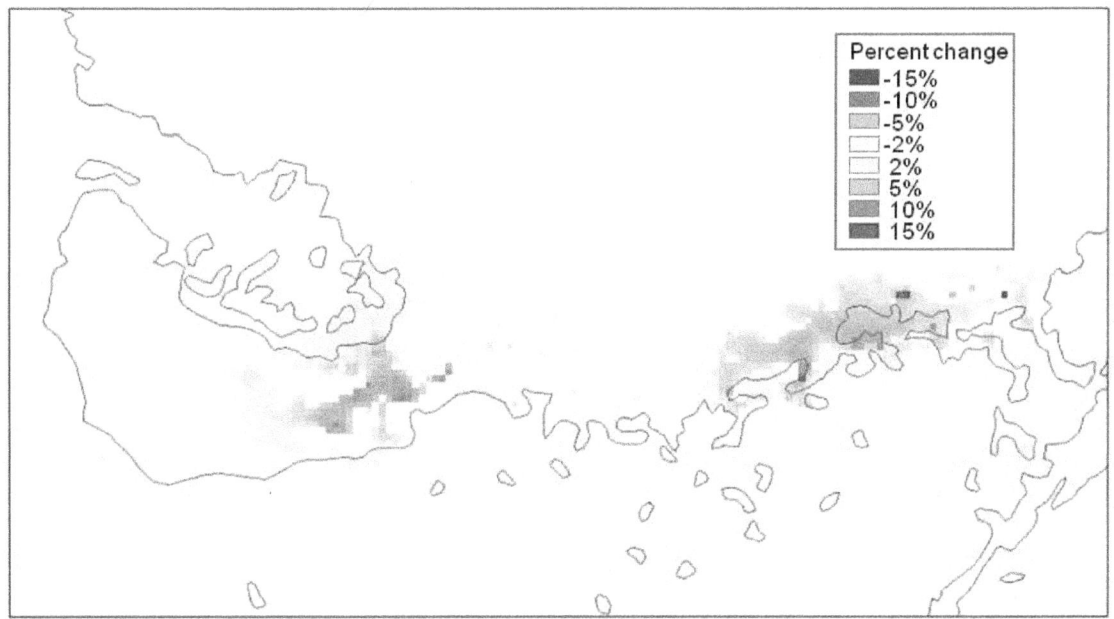

Figure 3-18. Percent change between American crocodile density and distribution under CERP0 conditions compared to CERP2050 conditions (Year 80).

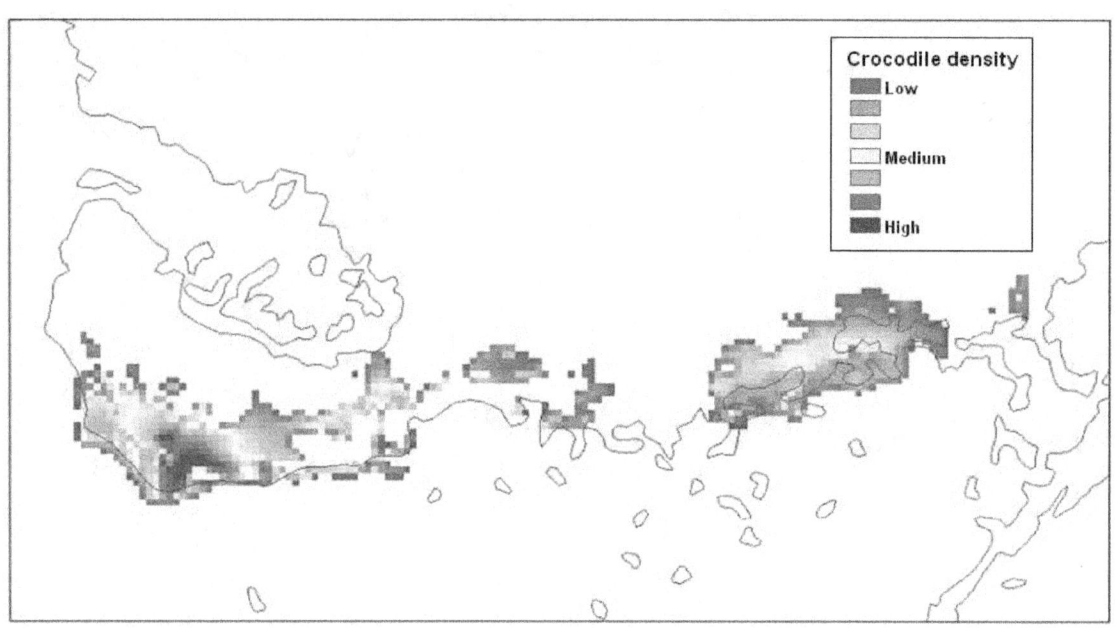

Figure 3-19. Hatchling American crocodile density and distribution under CERP0 conditions (Year 80).

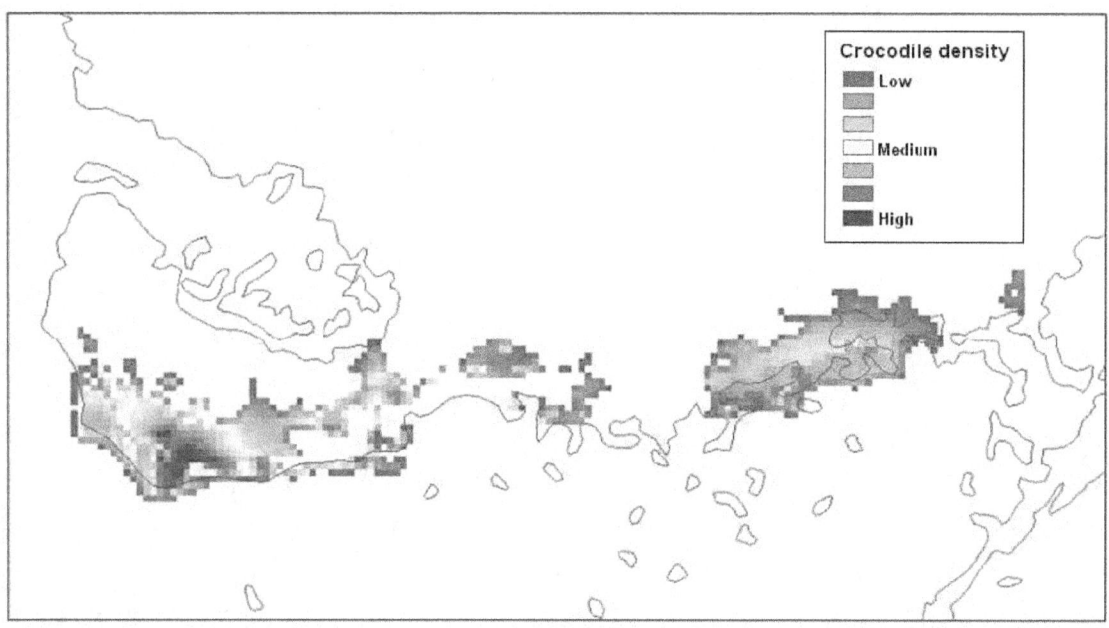

Figure 3-20. Hatchling American crocodile density and distribution under CERP2050 conditions (Year 80).

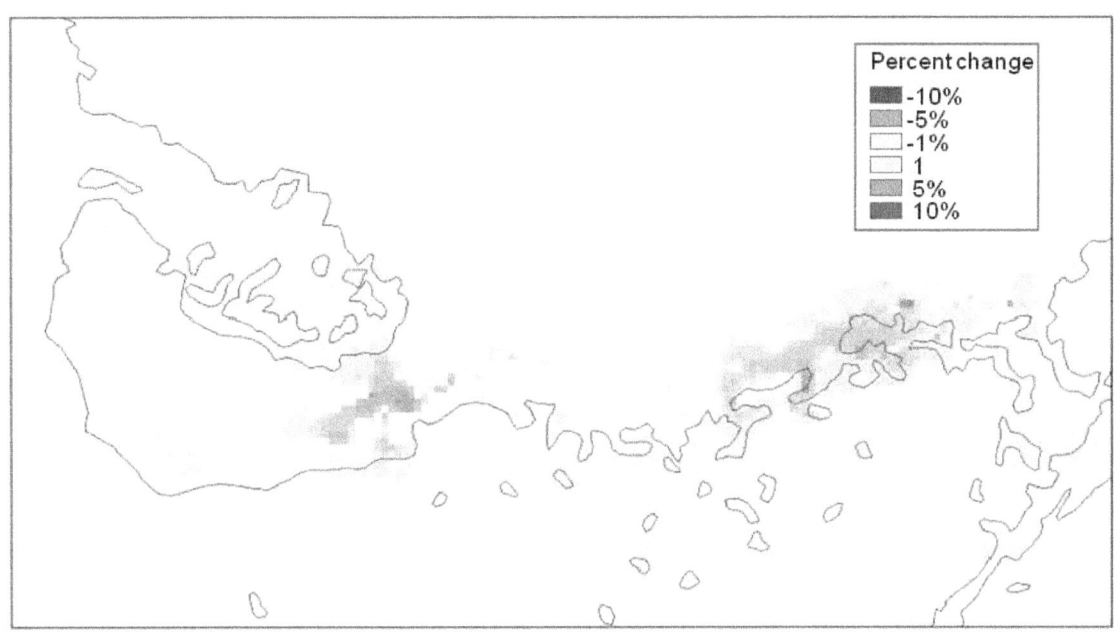

Figure 3-21. Percent change between hatchling American crocodile density and distribution under CERP0 conditions compared to CERP2050 conditions (Year 80).

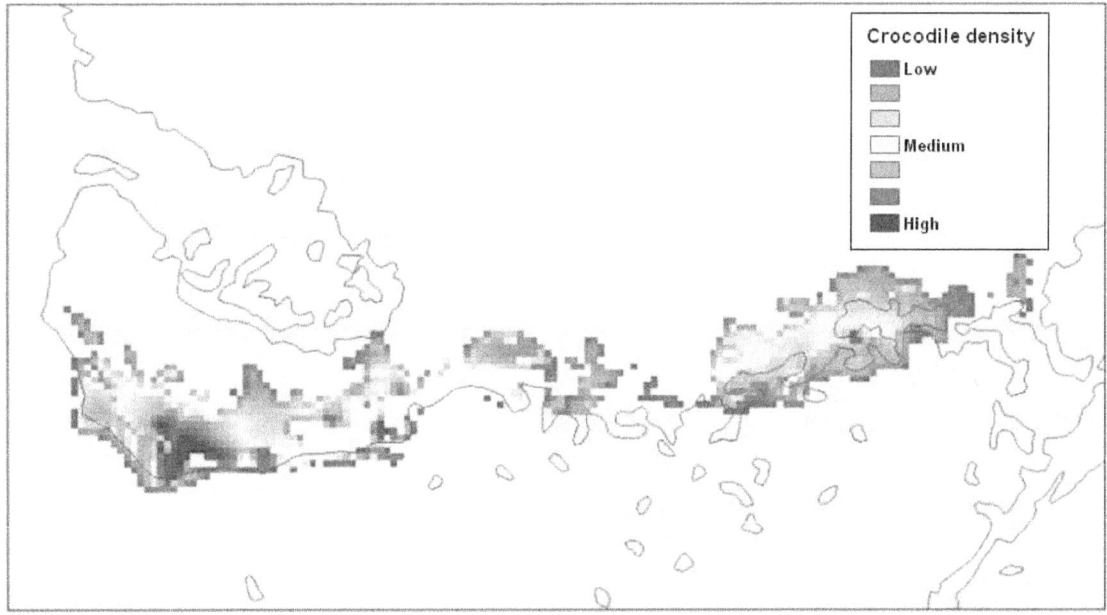

Figure 3-22. Hatchling and juvenile American crocodile density and distribution under CERP0 conditions (Year 80).

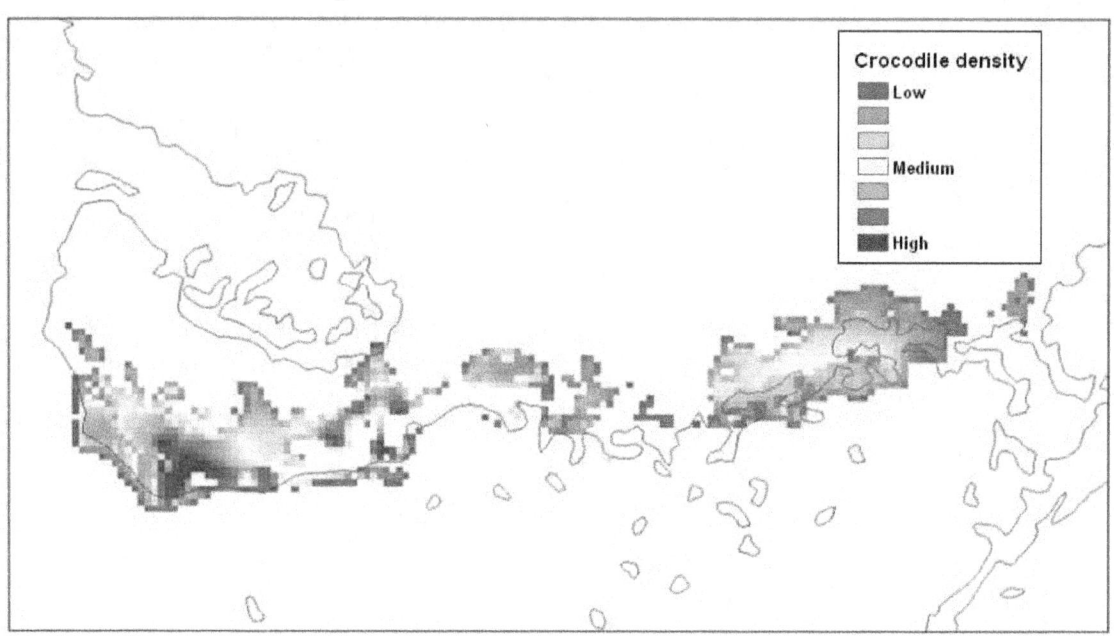

Figure 3-23. Hatchling and juvenile American crocodile density and distribution under CERP2050 conditions (Year 80).

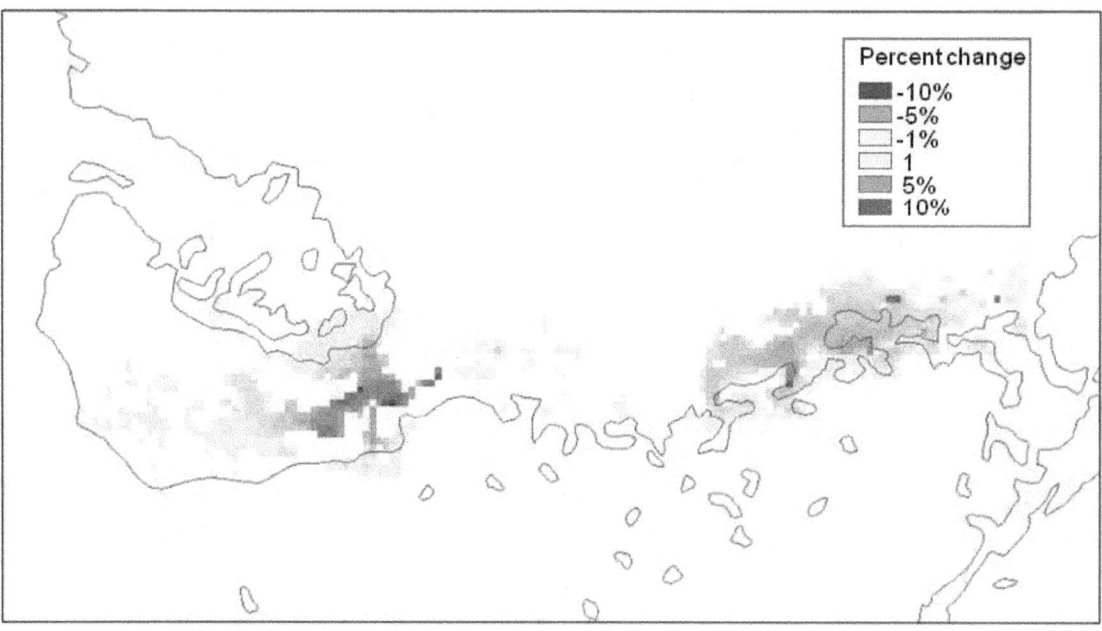

Figure 3-24. Percent change between hatchling and juvenile American crocodile density and distribution under CERP0 conditions compared to CERP2050 conditions (Year 80).

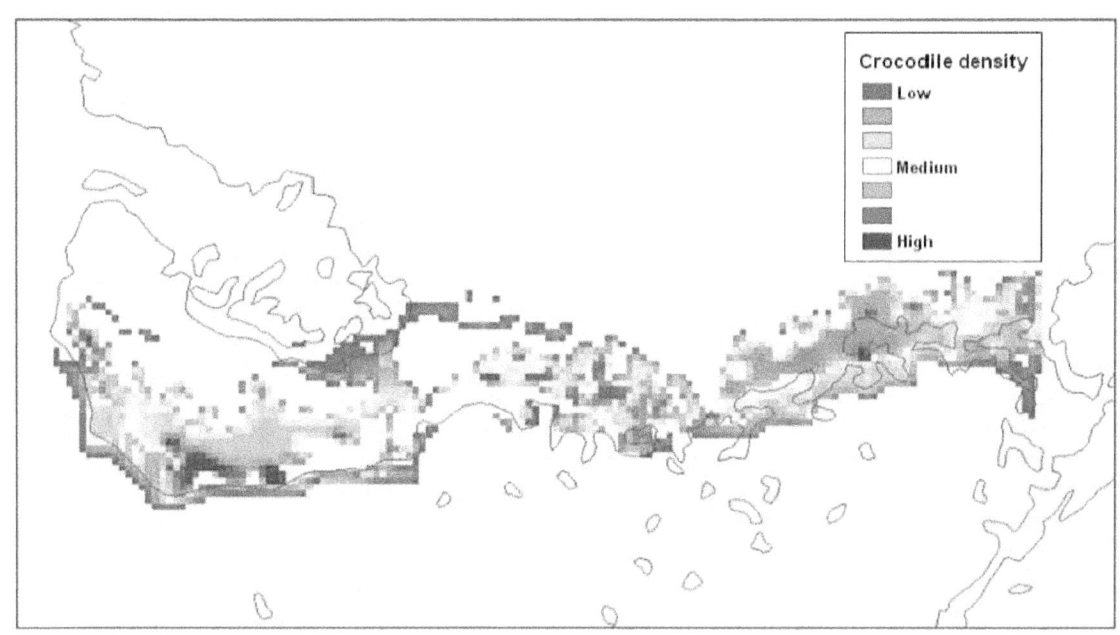

Figure 3-25. Subadult American crocodile density and distribution under CERP0 conditions (Year 80).

Figure 3-26. Subadult American crocodile density and distribution under CERP2050 conditions (Year 80).

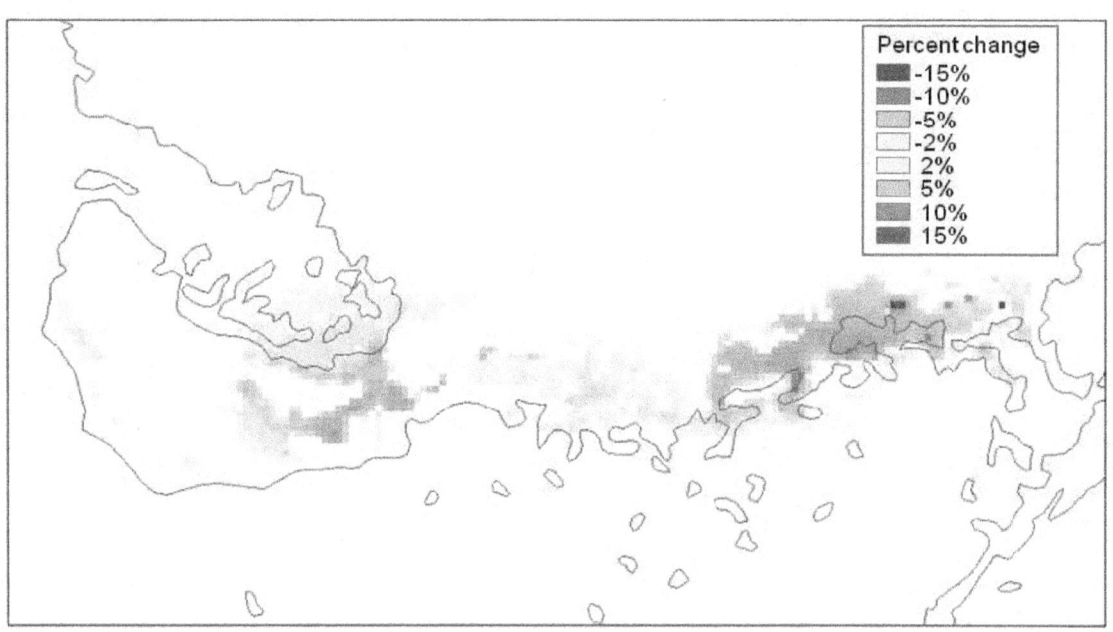

Figure 3-27. Percent change between subadult American crocodile density and distribution under CERP0 conditions compared to CERP2050 conditions (Year 80).

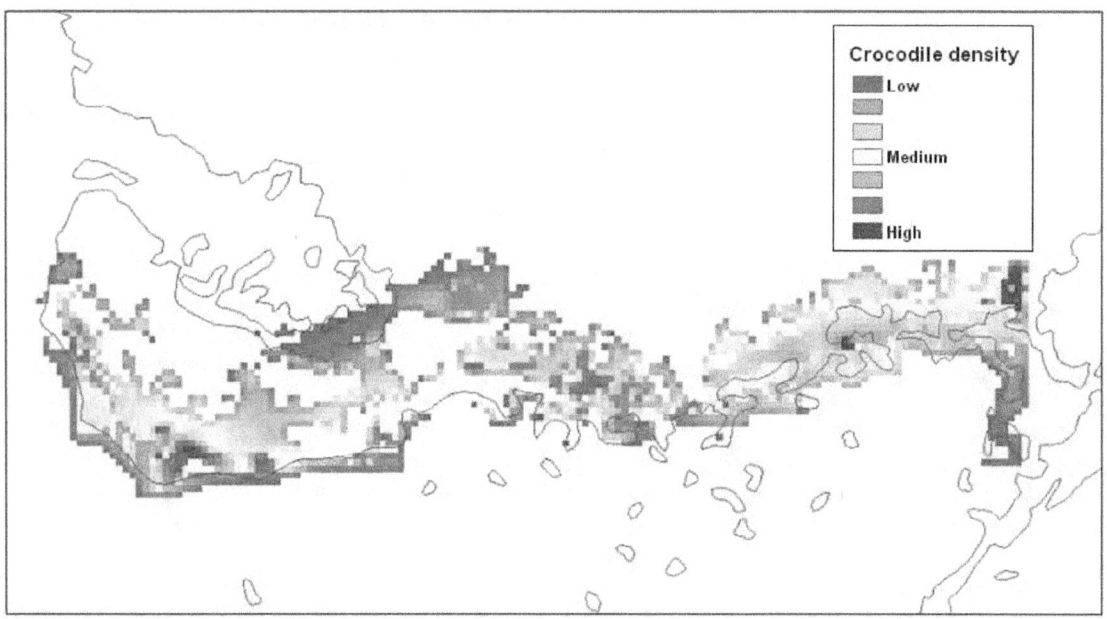

Figure 3-28. Adult American crocodile density and distribution under CERP0 conditions (Year 80).

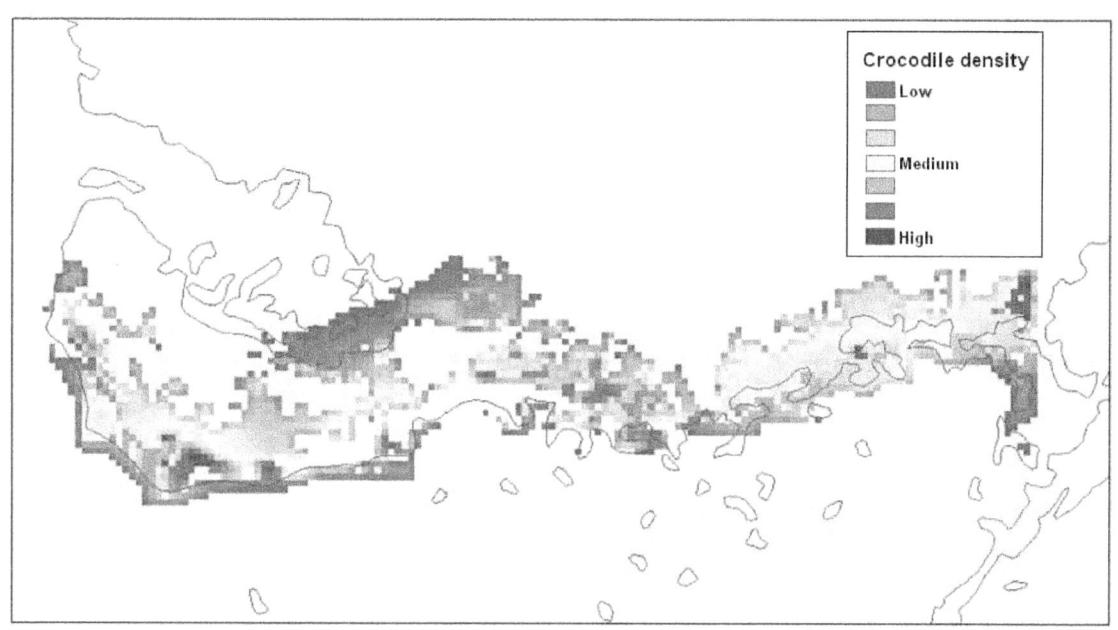

Figure 3-29. Adult American crocodile density and distribution under CERP2050 conditions (Year 80).

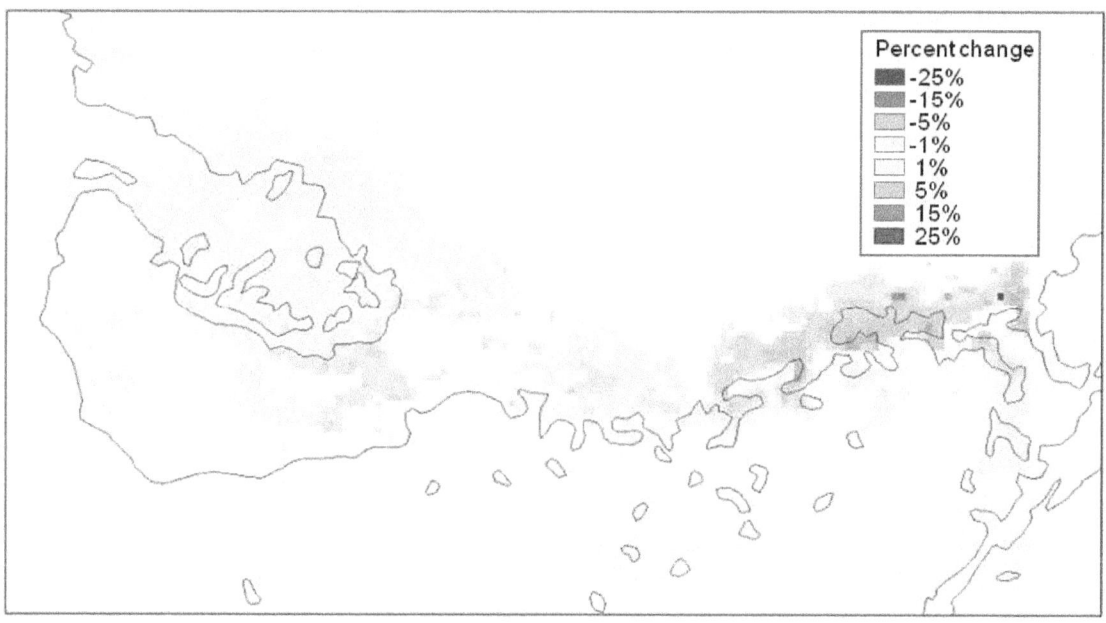

Figure 3-30. Percent change between adult American crocodile density and distribution under CERP0 conditions compared to CERP2050 conditions (Year 39).